THE THIRD CROWN

A Study in World Government Exercised by the Popes

Edmond Odescalchi

University Press of America, Inc.
Lanham • New York • Oxford

Copyright © 1997 by
University Press of America,® Inc.
4720 Boston Way
Lanham, Maryland 20706

12 Hid's Copse Rd.
Cummor Hill, Oxford OX2 9JJ

Library of Congress Cataloging-in-Publication Data

Odescalchi, Edmond P.
The third crown : a study in world government exercised by the popes /
Edmond Odescalchi.
p.   cm.
Includes bibliographical references and index.
1. Popes--Temporal power--History. 2. Church and state--Catholic
Church--History. 3. Europe--Church history--600-1500. I. Title.
BX1810.025 1997   262'.132--dc21   96-40107 CIP

ISBN 0-7618-0669-5 (cloth: alk. ppr)

To Esther, Daniel and Dominic

CONTENTS

ILLUSTRATIONS

PREFACE

There are a number of books, articles, and theses that discuss the pros and cons for the establishment of some kind of global authority to control the behavior of states. These treatises are all theoretical discussions. As far as I could determine there is no published work available that concentrates on the political history of the papacy, which was the only universal authority that actually exercised a measure of control over what we would call today sovereign states. This volume was conceived to fill that void. If we peek behind the curtains of the past, we may discern some lessons for the future.

I want to take this opportunity to thank a number of people who were of invaluable help in producing this book. I am indebted to my wife, Esther, for her help in researching the material; to Ellie Spain for using her artistic talents to do the sketches; to my son, Dominic, my daughter-in-law, Vida, Linda Smith, and Csaba de Szalay for their technical assistance. I also want to thank Dr. Paul Vesenyi, with whom I have discussed the concept for the monograph, and William Haiber who offered many helpful suggestions. I am also grateful to Dr. Istvan Lengyel, for allowing me to use his hideaway in sunny Florida to write a part of the book.

Edmond Odescalchi
Pleasant Valley, N.Y.
November 1996

Chapter 1:

The Concept of Global Authority

We are living in a world where it is practically impossible for any nation to exist in isolation. Countries are getting more and more interdependent. Wars fought with modern weapons of mass destruction are becoming increasingly self-defeating for the powers waging them and potentially destructive for the entire globe.

The 20th century has brought forth two devastating world wars, and after each an international organization to control the aggressive behavior of states was organized (the League of Nations, followed by the United Nations). They were created to arbitrate international disputes, control warfare, and maintain peace in the world.

Many people believe that this was a novel development in world history. If we look back across the centuries, however, we can see that in past ages the papal government acted as arbiter of the rulers of the world, and was the architect of the first supranational authority to control their behavior.

Nature abhors a vacuum. This is as true in world affairs as it is in physics. After the fall of the Roman Empire only the pope, heir of the mantle of leadership not only of St. Peter but also of Augustus, could fill that vacuum on the European scene. A cohesive society requires a set of shared values and behavioral norms of its members, and the papacy succeeded in making its values applicable to the world at large. Throughout the West, as his title implies, he was viewed as the common father of mankind.

The pope wears a triple crown. Although he is not crowned any more, it is still the symbol of his office. According to tradition, the first crown symbolizes the pope's territorial sovereignty over the Papal States (now reduced to the Vatican City); the second, his spiritual power over mankind; and the third, his moral authority over the kings of the world.

This book deals with the history of the third crown. It addresses exclusively the history of the papacy as a supranational authority over what we would call today independent and sovereign states. It examines the pope in his capacity of universal sovereign, who for centuries made and unmade the emperors and kings of Europe, and who divided the continents of the globe among European powers. This work does not discuss religion or ecclesiastical history, but world politics and international relations.

We have to realize, of course, that in centuries past the boundary between religion and politics was fuzzy or nonexistent. Ecclesiastical and secular spheres were intermingled at every level of society. Bishops and abbots sat in the assemblies of kings and often exercised territorial sovereignty over ecclesiastical principalities. And the reason for being of the Holy Roman emperor, the very purpose the pope created the imperial office, was to protect the Apostolic See and to promote its policies; although it is true that for much of history this was nothing but theory.

Even as late as the 16th and 17th centuries politics was still dominated by religious zeal and ideological fanaticism. During the wars of religion that followed the Reformation, there were no Capitalists, Communists, Conservatives and Socialists, only Catholics and Protestants fighting each other. Religion was perhaps the most powerful unifying and dividing force on the planet.

The papacy was so far the only power in the history of the world that established authority over what we would call today sovereign national governments. To be sure the Holy Roman emperor also claimed overlordship over the European commonwealth, but actual imperial authority never really extended beyond the boundaries of the empire. Only papal pronouncements made thrones shake and often fall a thousand miles away. The pope had the duty and the obligation, in the words of Innocent III, "not only the universal church but the whole world to govern" (Kelly 1986, 186).

The rulers of Europe recognized this papal preeminence. Pepin the Frank applied to the pope for authority to assume the royal crown. Alexius I of Byzantium petitioned the pope for help against the Turks (in response to which Urban II launched the crusades). When Columbus returned from his first voyage, the Spanish sovereigns asked the pope for a judgement on their global colonial claims.

The territorial rulers of the time recognized that the papal throne was the only supranational authority in the world. Only papal censures affected everyone and could be enforced everywhere, first only on the European scene and the Mediterranean basin, later, as the world came under European domination in the 15th and 16th centuries, throughout the globe.

When Leo III elevated Charlemagne to emperor of what later became known as the Holy Roman Empire; when Gregory VII deposed the German king, Henry IV; when Urban II launched the crusades; when Innocent II banned the crossbow as a weapon of war; when Alexander III arranged the peace between England and France; and when Gregory XIII ordered the reform of the calendar, the popes acted in their capacity of universal monarchs. Other rulers who applied to the sovereign pontiffs for a royal crown or for international arbitration implicitly recognized the papacy as the fountainhead of global legal power.

Today, the United Nations Organization performs many of the former functions of the papal government: bestowing legitimacy, allocating territories, censuring governments, ordering military operations, arbitrating conflicts, assuring the peace, and banning certain weapons.

In current political theory, sovereignty is vested in the people, who delegate authority to their elected magistrates. For much of human history, however, all power was said to have come from God and flowed down to the lowest official.

The pope's claim to overriding authority was based on the thesis that, by common consensus, he was the regent of God on earth. Only the pope could legally bestow the imperial crown, and only he and the emperor could create kings, and so on. As the fountainhead of imperial power, the pope stood at the summit of the feudal pyramid of the world.

In reviewing world history, we must look at the papal throne as the first and so far only supranational authority. As we shall see in this treatise, the papacy possessed all the requirements of a supranational world government:

-- A chief executive
-- Taxing authority
-- Armed forces
-- Enforceable laws
-- Courts of justice
-- Power over national governments
-- Global reach

Let us examine them one by one.

Chief Executive. The pope was chief executive with plenary powers. He headed the church's hierarchy because of the Petrine powers of binding and loosing. He was also the monarch of the Papal States, the fountainhead of imperial power in the Holy Roman Empire, and the feudal suzerain of many of the kingdoms of Europe. As vicar of God he claimed universal dominion over the globe.

Taxing Authority. As head of the church the pope imposed a tax directly on the people, known as the tithe, which amounted to about 10 per cent of the produce of the land. In addition to various rents and fees, certain countries had to send to Rome the Peter's pence, which consisted of a penny per household. Papal revenues were also derived from the Papal States and from the kingdoms that were vassals of the Apostolic See. The latter paid tributes that varied from case to case.

Armed Forces. In addition to the pontifical armed forces, kept for the defense of the Papal States, the pope had at his disposal the great military-religious orders of chivalry: the Templars, the Hospitalers, and the Teutonic Knights. These owed allegiance to the pope alone and fought his wars in Europe, the Middle East and North Africa. In addition, many secular rulers took up arms at different times at the pope's command.

Enforceable Laws. Based on decrees of councils and the fiats of popes, the papal government developed a legal system, known as the canon law. Since the church dominated life in the Middle Ages, canon law was enforced throughout western and central Europe. The pope exercised jurisdiction even over kings and emperors, especially in regard to their marital relations (and thus the legitimacy of their offspring) and the fealty of their subjects.

Courts of Justice. The papacy maintained its separate system of courts that decided cases dealing with marriages, wills, oaths, and those involving clergymen, widows, orphans, and crusaders. Even the civil court cases could be called into the papal court, which was the court of last resort.

Authority over National Governments. The pope awarded the imperial crown and raised other rulers to royal rank. He also claimed and often exercised the right to remove them from the throne. He censored governments, arbitrated conflicts, legitimized conquests, and annulled laws. In the words of Gibbon, "Thundering from the Vatican, he created, judged, and deposed the kings of the world" (Gibbon 1960, 857).

Global Reach. With the discoveries in the 15th and 16th centuries, papal jurisdiction finally attained global reach. The series of papal bulls of the 15th century in effect awarded America to Spain and Africa and Asia to Portugal. The kings of Spain always based the legitimacy of their rule in the Americas on the donation of Pope Alexander VI in the bull *Inter caetera*.

While the ancient Roman Empire existed, there was no need for an international organization, because the empire controlled the then known world. The prestige of Rome was such that the Eastern Roman emperors and the Holy Roman emperors both used the word "Roman" in their title for centuries after Rome became the capital of the Papal States and ceased to be a part of their empire.

An international system was first created by the papacy, which, by slow evolution, established a universal system of values through which it attained a sort of moral and legal ascendancy over individual rulers.

The most significant result of papal hegemony over secular rulers was that the papal throne united the feudal society of Europe into a commonwealth of nations, a kind of international state superimposed upon all territorial governments. As Gregory VII claimed at the council of Rome in 1080 the pope is empowered on earth "to take away and give empires and kingdoms" (Gontard 1964, 237), or as Boniface VIII said more than two centuries later, "through the apostolic see princes govern ... and kings rule" (Ullmann 1965, 128).

The pope did not claim to directly govern individual countries; he only insisted on moral leadership and the general supervision of the governments of the world. This was the essence of what the canon lawyers called *Regimen Universale* or world government.

Until the beginning of modern times, the papal government continued to operate even in the most unsettled times with a smoothness and efficiency derived of long experience. The papal government possessed a well organized machinery and an effective network of communication and control. Popes may be driven from Rome by insurrections, but their legates kept firm control in far away countries, like Germany, France, and England. Papal decrees may be flaunted by the warring factions of Rome, but they were obeyed and feared in the four corners of the known world.

This arrangement, in turn, was superseded by the modern concept of the sovereign state, which did not recognize a superior. Only in the 20th century, in the aftermath of two world wars, did the world realize the need for a global political structure for the purpose of containing international conflicts within moral and legal constrains.

The idea of nationhood dominates modern international relations. Its ascent started with the Renaissance but did not really reach its full flowering until the 18th century. Formerly rulers were by nature feudal, dynastic or theocratic. Before, the ideal was the universal world-state (Roman and Christian) not loyalty to a separate, parochial political body that nationalism represents.

Today the primary allegiance of people is to their nation. During the Middle Ages, however, the universal church headed by the pope was the only all-pervasive social reality. The lack of national feeling in earlier times is not surprising. In an era when dynastic interests determined policies, and when provinces were given away as dowries, nationalism took a long time to develop.

In discussing the past, I often use modern terms, like supranational, even though no nations in the modern sense may have existed at the time. The term simply means that an authority existed above territorial rulers whose domains today we would call sovereign states.

Also, no sharp distinction is made (although always mentioned) between the supranational acts of the papacy and those involving papal vassals, because the plenary powers of the pope were independent of feudal dependence. For example, when Pope Innocent III deposed King John, England was not a papal fief; the country became a vassal state of the Holy See only as a result of the papal action.

During the Middle Ages, ecclesiastical sanctions, implicitly believed in by the age, gave the pope a political advantage never previously enjoyed by one ruler over another. These conditions, we can say with certainty, will never recur. The power of a papal ban with deposition, on a supranational political level, was without precedent in history. It was the medieval equivalent of the atomic bomb, the most effective way to destabilize a government without sending in an invading army.

The papacy conceived of a world order based on the fusion of the universal claims of the Roman Empire and the Catholic Church. A shared concept of justice and a sense of legitimacy are the main prerequisites of an international order. These were institutionalized in the moral tenets of the papacy. They led to the recognition of the pope as international arbiter on a global scale.

Belief in their global mission enabled the popes to conduct their supranational policy with missionary zeal, using ideological, political, military, and economic weapons, until they seemed to tower over the international stage. For many centuries, it was only within the framework of the worldwide papal organization that the problems of the globe could be effectively addressed. As late as the 16th century, "popes still ratified treaties and received the 'obedience' of new sovereigns" (Encyc. Brit. 1963, s.v. "Papacy").

Perhaps by pondering the successes and the failures of the only supranational authority of the past, we may gain guidance for the future.

Chapter 2:

The Sweep of History

The Foundations of the Papal Monarchy

In 313 the Emperor Constantine I promulgated his edict of toleration making Christianity a recognized religion in the Roman Empire. After Constantine transferred his capital to the new city on the Bosporus in 330, and especially after Theodosius I declared Christianity the religion of the state in 380, the papacy necessarily became the focus of authority in West.

Long after the emperors had left for their new capital, the world kept looking to Rome for leadership, but there they saw a pope. In time papal Rome not only took the place of imperial Rome, but built a more extensive commonwealth than its predecessor ever possessed.

Pope Damasus I (366-384), as successor of St. Peter, claimed in accordance with the Petrine theory a unique juridical power "to bind and to loose" (in accordance with Matt. 16:18) in Roman legal terms. And Pope Siricius (384-399) was the first pope to issue decrees in the style of Roman imperial edicts, carrying the force of law.

Pope Leo I (440-461) was a cool-headed diplomat and the real ruler of Rome, now only an outpost of a shattered empire. He impressed the entire world when in 452 near Mantua he personally confronted Attila the Hun and persuaded him to spare Rome. Again in 455 he faced Gaiseric the Vandal outside Rome and, while he did not succeed to make him withdraw, he induced the Vandal chieftain to spare the citizens of the customary fire, torture, and massacre.

The doctrine of the two swords, which played such a prominent role in medieval political theory, was first expounded by Pope Gelasius

(492-496) in a letter to the Emperor Anastasius. According to this thesis God created two swords to rule mankind; the spiritual and the temporal, one wielded by the pope, the other by the emperor. By the 12th century, however, the canon lawyers asserted that both swords belonged to the pope, who delegated the temporal sword to the emperor (Clough 1969, 1:300).

The popes started early to embed their political philosophies in official documents and to project them through appropriate ceremonies. The reign of Pope Symmachus (498- 514) produced the first ruling that no human court could sit in judgment of a pope (Kelly 1986, 51).

John I (523-526) was the first pope to visit Constantinople, where the Emperor Justin prostrated himself before St. Peter's vicar and performed the ceremonial kissing of the pope's feet.

After these precedents, the civil authority of the papacy continued to grow. In 554 the Emperor Justinian, through his "pragmatic sanction," increased the temporal power of Pope Virgilius (537-555), giving him a voice in the appointment of the governors of the provinces and in the control of their finances. Virgilius's successor, Pelagius I (555-561) greatly increased this authority, organizing the temporal government of the Roman province, and making great strides on the road to political sovereignty.

Because of the breakdown of civil authority, Gregory I (the Great), who ruled from 590 to 604, laid the foundation of the future papal state. He dealt with foreign powers, negotiated treaties and appointed generals. He also reorganized the vast estates of the papacy in Italy, Sicily, Dalmatia, Gaul and North Africa, and took responsibility for feeding the people. Under him St. Augustine was sent to England.

As Byzantine power waned in Italy, only the papacy possessed a strong and vibrant organization to fill the void. Pope Gregory II, in 716, persuaded Liutprand, king of the Lombards, to relinquish papal lands he occupied, and even secured, in 729, his submission by having him deposit his royal insignia on the tomb of St. Peter. In the 8th century, the popes ceased to date documents by imperial years and began to strike their own coins.

All this increase in papal power was the product of natural political evolution brought about by the disappearance in 476 of a Roman emperor in the West. The pope instinctively stepped into the political vacuum thus created and assumed, not only in spiritual but also in temporal matters, the active leadership of Rome. Soon he was surrounded "with much of the pomp and semimystical ceremonial formerly reserved for the Emperors" (Norwich 1988, 174).

In spite of the rise of papal prestige, this state of affairs provided a rather precarious existence for the popes. Without large armed forces of their own, and with the Byzantine power in steady decline, it became imperative for the popes to find a powerful ally that could guarantee their security. They kept looking north of the Alps, and finally found what they were looking for.

In the middle of the 8th century, the Frankish monarchy was still ruled nominally by the impotent Merovingian dynasty. The effective governing power was Pepin the Short, the mayor of the palace. Pepin, however, was ambitious and intent on acquiring the royal sceptre, but in a legitimate way. Therefore, in 750, he sent am embassy to Rome, and asked Pope Zacharias for a judgment on who should be the rightful ruler of the kingdom.

Zacharias, in response to Pepin's appeal, delivered the momentous ruling that he who exercises the king's power should enjoy the king's title. Moreover, the pope, by his Apostolic authority, ordered Pepin to remove the feeble king, consign him to a monastery, and assume the crown himself. The Franks were absolved of their oath to the Merovingian dynasty (Gibbon 1960, 636).

Papal policy was always guided by the usefulness of a candidate for office. An incompetent king is useless in the furtherance of papal policies and, therefore, should be replaced by someone who is able to promote the papal program. Zacharias was a cultured and able administrator, who controlled the militia and government of Rome, and who boldly assumed the power to be the arbiter of sovereignty in the most powerful kingdom of the West. Pepin was duly anointed king, in Soissons, by the papal legate, Boniface.

The transfer of the crown to Pepin proved to have far reaching consequences, not only for the history of Europe, but also for the history of governmental ideas. Pepin needed legitimacy to supersede the Merovingian rulers, and this legitimacy was supplied by the papacy. Fifty years later "the secretary of Charlemagne affirms that the French sceptre was transferred by the authority of the Popes" (Gibbon 1960, 636). Thus, the world's first supranational authority came into being.

It was not long before Pepin had the opportunity to reciprocate the favor. When the next pope, Stephen II, was hard pressed by the Lombards, he appealed to the Frankish ruler for help. In 754 Stephen and Pepin met at the royal palace near present-day Chalons-sur-Marne. "When Pepin caught sight of the pope, he dismounted, knelt down and led the palfrey of Stephen" to his palace (Gontard 1964, 177).

After their conference Pepin immediately assembled his army and promised, in the so called "Donation of Pepin," to hand over ("restore") to the temporal dominion of the pope the former Byzantine Exarchate. Pope Stephen also reciprocated; he solemnly reanointed Pepin and, "in the monastery of St. Denis, placed the diadem on the head of his benefactor" (Gibbon 1960, 636). The pope also pledged to excommunicate all other potential claimants to the throne and, in addition, bestowed on Pepin the title of "Patrician of the Romans."

After defeating the Lombards twice, Pepin, as promised, surrendered the Exarchate, the Pentapolis, and Emilia to Pope Stephen. Thus, in 756, the Papal States came into being (to last until 1870) establishing the pope as a territorial sovereign.

The "restoration" to the pope of these territories was probably based on a document known as the Donation of Constantine, which in the 15th century was proved to be a forgery, but was very influential during the Middle Ages. According to this instrument the Emperor Constantine, when he transferred his capital to Constantinople, bestowed on Pope Silvester I the imperial insignia and the dominion of Rome, Italy and the western provinces. As we now know, the document was false, but the historical evolution was very real.

Pepin's successor, Charles the Great (Charlemagne), after capturing the Lombard capital, Pavia, and adding "King of the Lombards" to his titles, met Pope Adrian I in Rome and confirmed the donation of Pepin. In gratitude, the pope crowned Charlemagne's son, another Pepin, king of Italy, which kept the country from being submerged in the Frankish empire. (We have to remember, however, that the medieval kingdom of Italy comprised only the northern part of the peninsula. It did not include the Papal States and Naples and Sicily.) Adrian also crowned Charlemagne's other son, Louis, king of Aquitaine.

Although Charles was, in the words of Bertrand Russell, "dissolute in his life, and unduly fond of his daughters, ... he did all in his power to promote holy living among his subjects" (Russell 1945, 393). His relationship with the papacy was important to Charles, because he viewed Christianity as the glue that would hold the diverse races of his conquests together and give unity to his empire.

The pope who followed Adrian, Leo III, was plagued by the followers of his predecessor. He was violently attacked during a procession and a mob, according to some reports, cut out his tongue and gouged out his eyes. They couldn't have done a very thorough job, however, because when he appeared at the court of King Charles in Padeborn to ask for help he still had his tongue and eyes intact. His accusers followed him and charged him with perjury and adultery.

The king had Leo escorted back to Rome and followed him there a few months later. After Alcuin reminded King Charles that no man could sit in judgment of the Vicar of Christ, Leo was allowed to clear himself of the charges by oath. Whatever damage to his prestige the pope suffered through these proceedings, he regained it two days later by performing one of the fateful acts in world history, an act that set the political agenda for centuries, and that launched the papal throne on the way to universal political predominance.

The pope conceived and implemented a magnificent political program to establish the primacy of the papal government on the world stage. On Christmas day 800, when Charles rose from prayer at St. Peter's tomb, Pope Leo placed a crown on his head and proclaimed him, with the assembled audience, emperor of the Romans.

Leo boldly assumed the power to dispose freely with the highest office on earth, and established the precedent that only the pope can legally create a Roman emperor. It was an act that influenced the course of history for a thousand years. "Charles derived his claim of legitimacy from the Pope." From that time on, "no one could be emperor unless crowned by the Pope in Rome" (Russell 1945, 392).

Charlemagne's secretary, Einhard, reports that had the king known the intentions of the pope, he would never had set foot in St. Peter's church. The conferment of the imperial crown by the pope was indeed pregnant with danger for the emperor's successors.

Charles must have been aware that in Roman law he who can give can also take away, and therefore may have resented the papal initiative. If this, indeed, was the reason for the emperor's concern, history has proved him right. In the end, however, Charles had no choice but to accept with good grace the imperial crown as a gift of the pope.

Pope Leo had undoubtedly conferred a great honor on Charles the Frank, but "he bestowed a still greater one on himself: the right to appoint, and to invest with crown and sceptre, the Emperor of the Romans" (Norwich 1989, 379). By establishing the Roman (universal) imperial crown as a personal gift of the pope, he implicitly asserted his own superiority over the emperor, and raised the papal throne above all earthly rulers.

From the western point of view, the coronation in 800 did not create a second Roman Empire, because on the throne of Byzantium sat a woman, Irene (who called herself emperor, not empress) and according to Salic law no woman could wear a crown. In the eyes of both Leo and Charles, the imperial throne at that moment was vacant. In the 12th century, Innocent III could claim that in 800 the pope transferred the imperial crown from the Greeks to the Franks, and could transfer it again should he choose to do so.

By transferring the title from East to West, the pope signified that the ultimate power to bestow and to withdraw the imperial dignity rests with the pope. Here again, the pontiff acted in the capacity of a universal monarch. He did not conquer the Frankish kingdom (except with missionaries), neither was it, or the Roman Empire for that matter, a vassal state of the Apostolic See. Again, the pope acted, as he did when he transferred the royal power from Childeric to Pepin, as the world's first supranational authority.

Figure 2.1: Pope Leo III Bestows the Roman Imperial Crown on Charlemagne

Pope Leo III's diplomatic machinery was also effective in England, where skyrocketing papal prestige was instrumental in restoring King Eardulf of Northumbria to the throne.

Once initiated, the papal program was continued with single-minded determination. Leo's successor, Stephen IV, was welcomed in Rheims in 816 by Louis the Pious with elaborate ceremonial. In the cathedral the pope anointed Louis and crowned him emperor. Although Charlemagne had Louis crowned coemperor three years earlier, the ceremony at Rheims is a clear indication that in the eyes of contemporaries papal investiture was necessary for the legitimate exercise of imperial power.

The next pope, Paschal I, obtained from Louis guarantees (the *Pactum Ludovicorum*) of the possession of the Papal States, of no imperial interference in papal territories, and of the freedom of papal elections. In fact, this pact was somewhat ahead of the times, because later emperors did claim overlordship over the Papal States and did demand the right to confirm papal elections.

When Louis' son Lothair I went to Italy, the coronation ceremony was expanded to again amplify the papal theory of government. When Pope Paschal I crowned Lothair emperor, he also girdled him with a sword as a symbol of temporal power. This was the first time that the pope performed this procedure, which came to symbolize that the emperor is the strong arm of the papacy, and has the duty to protect the supreme pontiff and to enforce his policies. It became a salient feature of papal practice to always incorporate its program into a ritual that contemporaries understood.

The security of Rome naturally was always high on the papal list of priorities. To protect the city from the plundering Saracens, Pope Leo IV constructed walls on the right bank of the Tiber, creating the Leonine City, and for the first time enclosing St. Peter's within a defensive system. Going on the offensive he defeated the Moslems in a great sea battle off the coast of Ostia. In 850 he crowned Louis II, who was earlier crowned king of the Lombards by Sergius II, emperor at Rome.

The pope represented the memory of the worldwide organization of the Roman Empire and incorporated into his system the ideal of universal brotherhood taught by Christianity. As time went on, a papal commonwealth evolved and gave a political form to the unity of Christian Europe, which was the guiding idea of the Middle Ages.

As the Carolingian empire slipped further and further into chaos, the papacy grew to become the center of the state system of Europe. As the separate sovereignties arose out of the remnants of the Carolingian empire, these states were skillfully combined into a theocracy under the leadership of the sovereign pontiff.

The medieval world order found a strong representative in Nicholas I, who was firmly imbued with his position as God's vicar on earth. He forced King Lothair II of Lorraine to take back his wife and severely rebuked the Emperor Michael III of Byzantium for challenging the decrees of the Holy See. He greatly enhanced papal authority in the west, filling the vacuum created in 843 by the treaty of Verdun, which divided the empire among the sons of Louis I. (This gave birth to France and Germany as separate kingdoms.)

With John VIII the papacy made great strides in its ability to shape world events. He was an energetic pontiff who kept a strong hand at the helm. He personally led his troops against the Saracens, and launched a papal fleet to defend his states.

On the death of Louis II in 875, Pope John summoned Charles the Bald to take over the imperial office and crowned him in St. Peter's. After Charles' death, Carloman, son of Louis the German, demanded the imperial crown, but the pope refused to invest him. John VIII's choice fell first on Louis the Stammerer, whom he crowned emperor in 878 and, after his death a year later, on Charles the Fat, whom he recognized as king of Italy 879 and crowned emperor in 881.

Thus, in less than a hundred years after the coronation of Charlemagne, the papacy emerged as the effective arbiter of the imperial office, selecting and installing the emperor of the Romans. The popes used the imperial crown as an enticement with which they "dazzled the vanity of princes whom they summoned to their aid" (Bryce 1889, 82).

After these precedents, a king could not become emperor unless invested and crowned by the sovereign pontiff. Louis II was the first emperor who justified, in 871 in a letter to Constantinople, the legitimacy of his title by the fact that he had been crowned by the pope. "The role of the papacy as the agency which made emperors became one of its most treasured prerogatives" (Encyc. Brit. 1963, s.v. "Papacy"). It symbolized more than anything else the position of the pope as a supranational power, set above the nations and kingdoms.

Continuing the practice, Pope Stephen V awarded the empire to Guido of Spoleto and crowned him emperor in 891. Other shadowy emperors followed. Berengar of Friuli, crowned by John X in 915, was the last of the phantom emperors set up by the popes.

Finally the papacy realized that to enthrone these feeble emperors, who were incapable of giving it effective protection, was a useless exercise and gave up the practice. Just as the empire disintegrated, so, too, did the papacy experience the nadir of its history. Popes overthrew each other by force and died in dungeons.

During the so-called "pornocracy" the popes were either family members or pawns of the "Senator" Theophylact and his daughters Marozia and Theodora. Marozia, at 15, became the mistress of Pope Sergius III, and was the mother of John XI and the grandmother of John XII. Her sister Theodora was the mother of John XIII and of Benedict VI.

Marozia, who had her mother's lover, Pope John X, strangled in the Castle Sant'Angelo, soon ended up there herself. She was thrown into the dungeon of the castle by her own son, Alberic, "prince and senator of all the Romans," and spent the rest of her life there. Later the Crescentii family held sway in Rome, followed by the counts of Tusculum, whose dynasty included Pope John XIX, his brother Benedict VIII, and their nephew Benedict IX.

In spite of this state of affairs in Rome, popes still intervened to ensure legitimacy in Germany, France, and even beyond the Adriatic. The legate of John X presided over a synod at Hohenaltheim, in Germany, in 916, to prop up the tottering throne King Conrad I. Pope John X also bestowed the royal crown on Duke Tomislav of Croatia, in 925, raising the country to the rank of a kingdom.

A few years later, Stephen VIII intervened in France, in 942, on behalf of Louis IV, son of Charles the Simple, and forced the nobility of France and Burgundy, under threat of excommunication, to give up their revolt against the king (Kelly 1986, 124).

Under Agapitus II, the German king Otto first appeared in Italy and sent an embassy to the pope to ask for the imperial crown. Agapitus, who had excellent relations with Otto, nevertheless was forced by the political conditions in Rome to refuse the German king the imperial investiture.

The situation soon changed, however, after John XII (the grandson of Marozia) ascended the papal throne. When Berengar II, king of Italy, threatened the papal domain, it was now the pope who sent an embassy to Otto I of Germany, asking for military assistance and promising him the imperial crown.

The German king responded, defeated the pope's enemies and was crowned Roman emperor by a grateful John XII on the 2nd of February 962. Thus was reestablished the Holy Roman Empire that was to last in altered form until 1806. The pope soon found, however, that he had gained a master instead of a vassal. While the Papal State was extended to about two- thirds of Italy, the emperor also insisted on overlordship and a say in papal elections. A conflict became unavoidable and ended with the deposition and exile of the pope.

Although by his award of the imperial crown to Otto, John XII's impact on history was profound, he does not stand in very high regard in the church. He was an uninhibited and debauched youth in his twenties, and had perhaps the worst reputation among the popes of the pornocracy.

Pope John's lustful behavior had, in the words of Gibbon, "deterred the female pilgrims from visiting the tomb of St. Peter, lest, in the devout act, they should be violated by his successor" (Gibbon 1858, 5:61). John XII died as he had lived; he was said to have been slain by an outraged husband.

But the papacy proved resilient and soon rebounded under the tutelage of the German kings. Gregory V, the first German pope, was the cousin of Otto III, whom he crowned emperor in 996. The first German Pope was followed by the first French pope, Silvester II, a staunch champion of the traditional rights of the papacy. In 1001 he raised the Hungarian leader Stephen, of the house of Arpad, to royal rank, sending him the crown that is still the symbol of Hungary's national existence.

After him the Tusculani returned to power with Benedict VIII and John XIX. The latter crowned Conrad II emperor in 1027 in the presence of King Rudolph III of Burgundy and King Canute of England and Denmark. Two years earlier Pope John XIX also authorized the elevation of Boleslav I of Poland to royal rank, thus raising the country to the status of a kingdom.

With Henry III, the papacy definitely acquired a master, who installed and controlled several popes. Despite this temporary setback, however, the papacy continued to develop its ideology in the imperial coronation rites. Even at this time of imperial predominance, the only way for the German king to become Roman emperor was to go to Rome, take an oath of obedience to the pope and to kiss his feet. Only then could he receive the crown of the empire.

With Nicholas II, the actual situation began to change. Under the influence of the monk Hildebrand (later Pope Gregory VII), who was already pulling the strings behind the throne, the papacy took important steps to assure its independence and to create a feudal empire. The Lateran Synod of 1059 promulgated a new electoral law, placing the election of a pope in the hands of the College of Cardinals, shutting out all outside interference.

A few months later in the same year, at the Synod of Melfi, Pope Nicholas invested Robert Guiscard (son of Tancred of Hauteville) with the duchies of Apulia, Calabria and Sicily, and Robert of Aversa with the principality of Capua. The Norman leaders swore fealty to the pope and promised military assistance. Thus, with a stroke of the pen, Nicholas II extended papal overlordship over the entire southern half of the Italian peninsula.

By enfeoffing the Norman leaders, the papacy started a long practice of tying kings and princes to the Holy See by having them recognize papal overlordship. During the following centuries, many rulers placed their lands under the protection of the pope, to whom they promised military service and the payment of a yearly tribute. The practice was an effective way to stabilize a tottering throne at home, and in keeping hostile neighbors at bay. During the high Middle Ages the pope had more feudal vassals in Europe than any other power.

The year 1059 also saw the first papal coronation. The ceremony was never of religious significance; it was merely performed to show by suitable and concrete means the sovereign power and the truly monarchical character of the pope.

As a result of the steep increase in papal prestige, the rulers of the world began to apply to the papal court for arbitration of their conflicts. William the Conqueror sent a delegation under Gilbert of Lisieux to Rome in 1066 to ask Pope Alexander II for a judgment against King Harold of England for breach of oath. While there is no record of Harold being summoned to the papal court to defend himself, the sentence was evidently in William's favor, because the pope approved his invasion of England, and even sent him a consecrated papal banner for the undertaking.

As we have seen, out of the anarchy of the 10th century, the empire recovered first, and for a while overshadowed the papacy. But with the reform ideas originating in the Benedictine monastery of Cluny, the Apostolic See again recaptured its position as the most potent moral and political force in Europe. The reformers, imbued with the legal armory of papal pronouncements, including some false decretals, not only freed the papacy from the tutelage of the emperor, but turned the tables on the imperial power. From that time on, the German kingdom was on the defensive against the papal claims of universal dominion. With Gregory VII, the pope began his ascent to the sometimes dizzy heights of power. The age of the imperial papacy had begun.

The Imperial Papacy

The carefully shaped policies of earlier popes were finally translated into actuality in the reign of Gregory VII. He was a man of exceptional ability and determination, completely absorbed by the reform ideas originating in the monastery of Cluny.

The all-consuming goal of the policy of Gregory VII was to secure the independence of the church from the secular power, and in his view the only way to gain that independence was by asserting the supreme authority of the papal throne over the empire and thus over the state system of Europe. Pope Gregory was more than a fighter, he was the incarnation of an idea.

His program is expressed in 27 propositions of his *Dictatus Papae* that launched the two superpowers of the Middle Ages on a collision course. This document stated unequivocally papal supremacy over all earthly rulers, ecclesiastical as well as temporal.

In the document Gregory claimed, among other things, that the pope alone has the power to depose and reinstate bishops; that the pope alone may use the imperial insignia; that he has the power to depose emperors; that his decrees can be annulled by no one; that he can be judged by no man; and that he has the power to absolve the subjects of unjust rulers from their oath of allegiance.

Gregory embarked to make Europe into a theocratic state under papal predominance. Popes Nicholas II and Alexander II had already issued decrees against simony (the sale of offices), clerical marriage, and lay investiture (the right of lay rulers to invest with ecclesiastical offices).

Gregory immediately insisted on the implementation of those decrees. The ban on lay investiture naturally brought him into conflict with the German king, Henry IV. Bishops, archbishops, and abbots not only exercised spiritual jurisdiction, but their sway in the political sphere was overwhelming.

Many churchmen were temporal sovereigns   of ecclesiastical

and, during his feud with Henry IV, claimed the power "to take away and to grant empires, kingdoms, principalities, dukedoms,... and the possessions of all men according to their merits" (Sabine 1937, 235). He considered all mankind a single society under the supreme authority of the pope.

The investiture controversy was settled in France and England in a rather undramatic way. In both countries the kings abided by the papal decrees and renounced investiture, but retained the right to the bishops' allegiance for their temporalities. These agreements were ratified by Pope Paschal II.

It was left to Calixtus II to settle the quarrel over the investiture in the empire. He was the son of Count William of Burgundy and was related to the German, English and French royal families. After arduous negotiations the Concordat of Worms was signed on the 23rd of September 1122. The emperor renounced the right to invest with ring and crozier, but retained the privilege of investing with the temporalities, symbolized by the scepter.

In Germany, temporal investiture was to precede the spiritual; in Italy and Burgundy, the spiritual investiture was to precede the temporal. The concordat, of course, did not extend to the Papal States, where the pope was both temporal and spiritual sovereign.

In the words of James Bryce, "the Papacy remained master of the field." The emperor came out of the struggle "with tarnished glory and shattered power" (Bryce 1889, 163). The compromise of Worms changed the old system, freed the papal organization from secular influence and, as later history shows, started the process of turning it into a superstate. The concordat settled the question of investiture, but not the underlying issue of the superiority of the two world powers. The next century saw the monarchical authority of the pope over the West reach the apogee of its development. The desire of the German kings for the imperial crown, which only the pope could bestow, drew them unavoidably into the vortex of the papal theory of government with its claim of hegemony over the crowns of the world.

A worthy successor of Gregory VII was Urban II, who firmly anchored the military leadership of Europe to the papal throne. In 1095, as the Turks were assaulting the frontiers of the Eastern Empire, Pope Urban received an urgent appeal for military assistance from the Emperor Alexius I Comnenus.

The pope responded by making, at the Council of Clermont, one of the most influential speeches in the history of the world. He called on all Christians to unite in a great military undertaking, known as the crusades, to conquer the Holy Land and to relieve the military pressure on the Eastern Empire.

Here again, the Byzantine emperor implicitly recognized the pope as the head of the European state system and as an international authority who exercised control over the western world. By applying to the pope and not to the western emperor or the kings of Europe, Alexius acknowledged that only the pope had the universal authority to unite the West and to launch a military undertaking of a magnitude required to save his empire.

At the council, the pope also extended the Truce of God to all of Europe. The Truce of God was an instrument for peace used by the popes to restrict feudal warfare to certain days of the week. Urban realized that before uniting the continent for such a vast undertaking against a common external enemy, he had to ensure peace among the warring kings of Europe.

With our 20th century mentality, we may be puzzled by the wave of enthusiasm sparked by his words, as Europe turned into a vast army under the leadership of the pope. Even Urban was overwhelmed by the response to his call to arms. Soon a stream of humanity was moving down across the Balkans in pursuit of a holy mission. After a bloody and savage but victorious campaign the crusaders took Jerusalem by storm on the 15th of July 1099.

The leadership of the crusading movement gave a tremendous boost to the political prestige of the papacy. In Germany, papal power grew to such an extent that it determined the choice for the royal crown. Pope Honorius II supported Lothair II, who became the first German king to ask for papal approval of his election. In 1128 Honorius also recognized Roger II as duke of Apulia and received his oath of fealty.

Even while papal prestige skyrocketed, the Romans were as unruly as ever. Honorius' successor, the Papareschi pope, Innocent II, induced King Lothair II, by promising him the imperial crown, to wrest Rome from the antipope "Anacletus II." When this was accomplished in 1133, the Pope crowned Lothair emperor, but in the Lateran, because Anacletus still held out in the Leonine City.

Innocent II also enfeoffed the new emperor with the vast lands of the Countess Matilda of Tuscany, which had been a bone of contention between the papacy and the empire. In 1131, at the synod of Rheims, the pope also crowned Louis VII, the heir of Louis VI of France, who was already associated with his father in governing the country.

In Germany Conrad III, the first Hohenstaufen, owed his election in 1138 to the legate of Pope Innocent II and the ecclesiastical electors. Since the election was challenged, the king "was forced to admit the necessity of appeal to Rome and to acknowledge the supremacy of the papal decision (Encyc. Brit. 1953, s.v. "Papacy").

From the east, however, came bad news. In the crusader states, Edessa fell in 1144 and created great consternation in Europe. In response to the calamity, Pope Eugenius III (Bernardo Paganelli) launched the Second Crusade, led by King Louis VII of France and King Conrad III of Germany.

When Conrad died, his successor, Frederick I Barbarossa, announced to the pope his election as German king. In 1153 Pope Eugenius III concluded with him the treaty of Constance, promising him the imperial crown in return for military help against the turbulent Roman commune.

By the time Frederick appeared in Rome for his imperial coronation, however, Pope Eugenius was dead and Adrian IV (Nicholas Breakspeare) sat on the throne of St. Peter. The only English pope in history, he was a bold and forceful character, determined to live up to the full monarchical claims of the papacy.

At their first meeting in Sutri in 1155, the German king made no secret of his displeasure of having to perform the courtesies that made him appear as the pope's vassal. But Adrian insisted on the traditional ceremony. For him it was not mere quibbling over protocol; it was a public recognition of the proper relationship between the two powers.

It was the king who finally blinked. He wanted the imperial crown and knew that only the pope could bestow it. Two days later the meeting was repeated:

> This time the King advanced on foot to meet the Pope, took his horse by the bridle and led it the distance, we are told, of a stone's throw; then holding the stirrup, he helped him dismount (Norwich 1995, 109).

Ever since the meeting in Sutri, the relationship of the two sovereigns was strained. The seeds of dissension had been sown. When Pope Adrian IV died, Frederick realized that he must control the papacy, if he was to establish his sway over Italy, but he went about it in a rather inept way.

As Adrian's successor, Alexander III (Orlando Bandinelli) was being enthroned, Cardinal Octavian, the candidate of Frederick, tried to snatch the papal mantle off his back and, after an unseemly tug-of-war, made a dash for the throne (Norwich 1995, 3:132). In spite of this less than edifying performance, the emperor deemed it a legitimate way of attaining the papacy and recognized his nominee as "Pope Victor IV."

After these antecedents, it is not surprising that under Alexander III, the first of the great lawyer popes, the breach with the empire came to a head. The contest ended with the decisive defeat of Emperor Frederick I at the battle of Legnano in 1176 by the forces of the Lombard League, allies of the pope.

The emperor was forced to submit to the legitimate pontiff. A scene almost like Canossa repeated itself in Venice, and enshrined the triumph of the papacy. On the 15th of July 1177,

> Alexander took his seat on the throne in front of St. Mark's. Approaching him in solemn procession, the Emperor took off his purple cloak, prostrated himself and kissed the Pope's feet. Alexander raised him up, embraced him and gave him his blessing (Cheetham 1982, 121).

Recognition of the pope's universal preeminence was not restricted to the West. In 1166, the Byzantine emperor, Manuel I Comnenus, attempted to induce Alexander III, by offering him ecclesiastical, political, and financial inducements, to crown him universal emperor, thus uniting the Western and the Eastern Empires. (Frederick I had been under the papal ban since 1160.) The pope must have been flattered to receive the acknowledgment of his global power over empires and kingdoms from such an unlikely quarter, but naturally nothing came of the project.

The Byzantine emperor again hoped for salvation for his empire from the pope. The news from the Middle East spelled one disaster after another. After the battle of Hattin in 1187, Jerusalem fell to Saladin, and Pope Gregory VIII (Alberto de Morra) immediately launched the Third Crusade to reconquer it.

The apogee of the imperial papacy was undoubtedly the rule of Pope Innocent III (Lothario de Conti, son of the count of Segni), which lasted from 1198 to 1216. He was only 37 years old and not even a priest at the time of his election by the unanimous vote of the College of Cardinals.

A born ruler, he combined intelligence, determination, and strength of character. Reflecting his views, he started his pontificate with a sermon citing the Biblical passage (Jer. 1:10), "See I have this day set thee over the nations and over the kingdoms ... to destroy and to pull down, to build and to plant" (Clough 1969, 1:302).

The Emperor Henry VI having died a year before, Innocent immediately took steps to fill the power vacuum. He strengthened his authority in the Papal States, which had been slipping away under his predecessors, and reestablished papal overlordship over the kingdom of Sicily.

He also claimed special rights in Germany, because the German king, after coronation by the pope, became emperor of the Holy Roman Empire and thus the secular arm of the papacy. Innocent firmly embraced the theory of papal hegemony over the kingdoms of the world, and made it a reality.

Henry VI's death was followed by a disputed election between Otto of Brunswick and Philip of Swabia. The candidates themselves as well as the imperial electors appealed to the pope for arbitration. Thus, the German princes again recognized the papacy as an international arbitral power. The pope, in a decision handed down in 1201, awarded the empire to Otto.

In the contested election in Germany, Innocent convincingly marshals the arguments from the point of view of papal theocracy:

> the pope as vicar of Christ, the true Priest-King, confers imperial power to which no claimant has a right, for it is only through the exercise of papal favor that a king can be promoted to emperor. The idea of papal universal monarchy had never been so trenchantly exposed and applied as in these and similar pronouncements of Innocent III (Encyc. Brit. 1963, s.v. "Papacy").

In 1209 Otto IV received from the hands of Innocent III the imperial crown, but soon disappointed his patron. In spite of his promises to respect papal sovereignty over central Italy, he invaded the papal territories and lay claim to the papal fief of Sicily. Thereupon Innocent III excommunicated and deposed the emperor only one year after his coronation (Otto was defeated at Bouvines in 1214) and promoted his ward, Frederick of Hohenstaufen, to the imperial throne.

Frederick II, who through his mother was also heir to the kingdom of Sicily, had to accept the pope's condition that the German and Sicilian crowns be never united on a single head. He formally renounced the throne of Sicily in favor of his infant son, Henry (who later rebelled against his father and died a prisoner). The pope was very much aware of the danger of letting the Papal States be squeezed in a geopolitical vise.

Innocent also had a serious feud with King John of England over the appointment to the see of Canterbury. The pope first excommunicated John and placed the country under the interdict. When this did not have the desired effect, he finally, in 1213, formally deposed the king from the throne of England and commissioned Philip II (Philip Augustus) of France to execute the sentence.

In the end, John was forced to submit and to surrender his crown to the papal legate. As the king stated in his official letter: "We offer and freely yield ... to our lord Pope Innocent III and his catholic successors, the whole Kingdom of England and the whole Kingdom of Ireland" (Lyon 1964, 111). After this complete surrender, John was reinstated by the pope as a vassal of the Holy See. The king acknowledged his new status and promised to "bind in perpetuity our successors and legitimate heirs that without question they must render fealty ... to the Supreme Pontiff" (Lyon 1964, 11).

In addition to England, Aragon, Portugal, Poland, Hungary, Sicily, and Bulgaria acknowledged the pope as their feudal suzerain.

Pope Innocent III also exercised active leadership in the military affairs of the European commonwealth, although it can not be claimed that he also kept control. He launched the Fourth Crusade in 1202 which, against his will, was diverted to Constantinople, where the crusaders set up the Latin Empire. In the end, however, the pope accepted the accomplished fact and ratified the conquest.

Another crusade launched by Innocent III was the one against the Albigensian sect in the south of France in 1208. He tried for many years to arrive at a peaceful solution, and ordered the use of military force only as a last resort. The pope was much concerned with the maintenance of ideological purity throughout Europe. In his view, it would have been pointless to extend the geographic frontiers of the Papal Commonwealth if within the continent the political cohesion of society would have been allowed to disintegrate.

The highlight of Innocent's pontificate was the Fourth Lateran Council in 1215. It was really a parliament of Christendom, attended by representatives of the Western and Eastern emperors and all the kings of Europe, presided over by the pope, the supreme director of all the spiritual and political affairs of the world.

Figure 2.2: King John of England Surrenders his Crown to the Papal Legate

Because the Fourth Crusade never reached the Holy Land, at the Lateran council the pope proclaimed the Fifth Crusade. He also listened to rival claimants to the empire and formally awarded the throne to Frederick of Hohenstaufen. The judgement enshrined the final authority of the papacy over the empire.

Innocent III firmly believed in the universal monarchy of he papacy, and his authority went unchallenged by contemporaries. He claimed the power of supervision over all countries and therefore considered himself the supreme judge in conflicts among national governments.

In his view, papal powers did not apply to Christians only, but to all the inhabitants of the globe. As he stated to the ambassadors of Philip Augustus of France, the pope is the vicar of the Creator and his authority encompasses "the whole wide world and all that dwell therein" (Encyc. Brit. 1953, s.v. "Innocent").

In spite of these statements, however, Innocent did not strive for the actual government of the world. He was quite content to let the secular authorities do their work. He was prepared to intervene only when he was owed allegiance as in the papal and vassal states, where moral or spiritual issues required his interference, or in cases where there was no superior arbiter; in other words, what we would call today a supranational world authority.

Innocent III was not the creative, fiery genius as Gregory VII, but a cool and calculating statesman who never missed an opportunity to extend the papal power. When contemplating an action, he always asked three key questions: Is it beneficial? Is it lawful? and Is it feasible? Some of his successors in later centuries should have remembered the third question.

The real proof of the pope's universal authority was the fact that he was not required, like the emperor or a king, to send armies to distant parts of the world to enforce his decrees. It took only a flip of the papal pen to make a throne totter a thousand miles away. Kings were limited by locality; in fact, their title could not be separated from the territory they possessed. Papal sovereignty, on the other hand, was irrespective of the land; it was over people and the whole earth.

Based on the accomplishments of Gregory VII, Alexander III, and especially Innocent III, the popes of the 13th century continued to exercise their hegemony over the European state system.

Because King John of England became a vassal of the Holy See in 1213, the Savelli pope, Honorius III, compelled France to abandon the invasion of the country. In 1223 the pope allowed Henry III, who was still a minor, to mount the throne of England by declaring him of age. In France Louis IX succeeded, with the help of the papal legate, in thwarting a rebellion and assumed the throne in 1226. (He is known as St. Louis, who later led the Seventh and Eighth Crusades.)

In the empire, on the other hand, shadows of future troubles began to appear. When the German King Frederick II came to Rome in 1220, and renewed his promise to go on a crusade, Pope Honorius III crowned him emperor of the Holy Roman Empire. But Frederick proved to be a lukewarm crusader, who did not completely tow the papal line.

To fire up the emperor's enthusiasm, the pope even arranged his marriage with Isabella de Brienne, heiress to the kingdom of Jerusalem. When the emperor still procrastinated he got into a sharp conflict with the next two popes, Gregory IX (Ugolino de Conti di Segni, nephew of Innocent III) and Innocent IV (Sinibaldo Fieschi, son of the count of Lavagna).

Pope Gregory IX distrusted the emperor and was clearly sceptical of the imperial motives. The papal wars against Frederick II started in 1228, when Gregory IX repelled incursions of imperial troops into papal territories, and launched the papal armies under the command of John of Brienne against the possessions of Frederick II in the south of Italy.

Although the emperor defeated the papal forces, he realized that in order to consolidate his gains and secure his rule he needed to free himself of the papal ban. The antagonists effected a reconciliation at Ceprano in 1230. The emperor promised to respect the territorial integrity of the Papal States and the pope lifted the ban. But the truce proved only temporary. When the emperor made another attempt to reduce Italy, the fight was renewed.

In 1239 Pope Gregory IX again excommunicated Frederick and proclaimed a crusade against him in Germany and Italy. Crusaders in Hungary were allowed to commute their vows to fight against the emperor.

Pope Innocent IV, who ascended the papal throne in 1243, followed the policy of his predecessors. Although an attempt was made for a peaceful resolution of the conflict, the situation soon deteriorated because of imperial designs on Lombardy. Frederick was again placed under a papal ban and was ordered to appear before the Council of Lyons in 1245 to answer charges of perjury, breach of peace and heresy. He did not appear in person, but was represented and defended by Thaddeus of Suessa.

The emperor's efforts were in vain. Pope Innocent IV, an expert in the art of political maneuver, ignominiously stripped Frederick of his dignities of Holy Roman emperor and king of Sicily, released his subjects from the their oath of fealty, and renewed the crusade against him. The pope, of course, did not recognize the emperor's son Conrad IV, and invited the German princes to elect a new king.

Under the leadership of the three Rhenish archbishops, the electors first chose Henry Raspe of Thuringia, and after his death in 1247, William II, count of Holland, to fill the vacant throne. The conflict finally ended with Frederick's death in 1250.

The popes prevailed over the emperors because they possessed both temporal and spiritual weapons in their armory. "The power of the keys claimed to prevail, not only in this world, but beyond the grave" (Binns 1995, 54). While the kings of France and England slowly consolidated their power and established centralized states, the German kings spent most of their energies challenging the popes for the dominion of the world.

With the fall of the Hohenstaufen, the Papal Monarchy triumphed over the empire, but its victory was won at a ruinous cost.

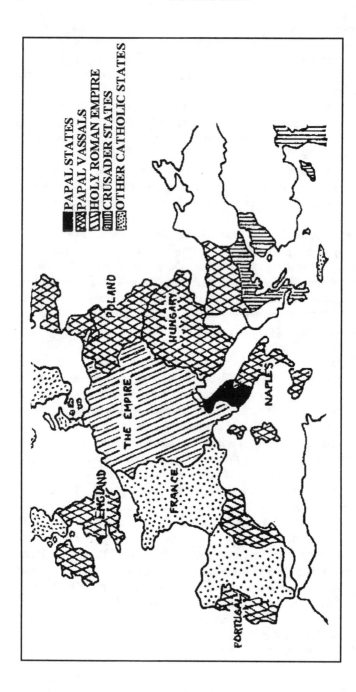

Map 2.1: The Papal Commonwealth in the High Middle Ages

By employing spiritual weapons for political ends, criticism of the papacy's tactics mounted, and its prestige suffered in the process.

The pope was especially concerned with the kingdom of Sicily, which was a feudal fief of the Holy See. After deposing Frederick, Pope Innocent IV offered the crown of Sicily to Edmund, son of Henry III of England, and even contemplated annexing the country to the Papal States. Edmund was actually enfeoffed with the kingdom by Pope Alexander IV (Rinaldo Conti di Segni) in 1255, but since he could not shoulder the military and financial burdens associated with this "gift," the arrangement was liquidated three years later.

The crisis in the southern kingdom came to a head under Pope Urban IV (Jacques Pantaléon), who in 1263 awarded the crown of Sicily and Naples to Charles of Anjou, brother of Louis IX of France. The prince accepted the kingdom as a fief of the Holy See, agreed to pay 50,000 mark sterling, promised an annual tribute of 10,000 ounces of gold, and committed himself to extend military assistance to the pope when needed. He was required to take possession of the kingdom within one year.

In Germany, Urban IV naturally prohibited the election of Conradin of Hohenstaufen, grandson of Frederick II, but did not decide on any of the two contending candidates for the imperial throne, although both Richard, earl of Cornwall, and Alfonso X, king of Castile, acknowledged his right of arbitration.

Meanwhile in Italy Charles of Anjou entered Rome in 1265 and was invested by commission of Pope Clement IV (Guy Foulques) with the kingdom of Naples and Sicily. When Conradin tried to take over the kingdom, Clement excommunicated him and deposed him from the throne of Jerusalem. Conradin was eventually defeated and captured by Charles at Tagliacozzo in 1268.

Clement IV, who claimed suzerainty over the empire and therefore the right to take over the government during a vacancy, also named King Charles imperial vicar in Italy. It was in that capacity that Charles had Conradin, the last of the Hohenstaufen, executed as a disturber of the peace. While the popes continued to dispose of the crowns of the world, they realized, only too late, that in Charles of Anjou they had created a mighty threat to their hegemony.

The fall of the Hohenstaufen continued to reverberate in Germany. After the death of Richard of Cornwall, the Visconti pope, Gregory X, did not recognize the claims of Alfonso X of Castile, and in spite of the pressure of Charles of Anjou refused to support the candidacy of Philip

III of France for the imperial throne. Maintaining the balance of powers was always a prime consideration of papal policy.

Finally, faced with dwindling revenues from an anarchy- infested Germany, and fearing the growing power of Charles, Pope Gregory X called on the German electors to choose a king. If they failed to do so, the pope threatened to name an emperor. The German princes obeyed Gregory, and elected his hand-picked candidate, Rudolph of Habsburg.

After Rudolph satisfied all the pope's demands, Gregory X, at the Council of Lyon in 1274, proclaimed Rudolph king of the Romans, and invited him to Rome for the imperial coronation, scheduled for the 2nd of February 1276. The pope, however, died before that date and, in spite of later attempts, Rudolph never attained the imperial diadem.

At the Council of Lyon, Gregory X also proclaimed a crusade to the Holy Land, and received the submission of Michael VIII of Byzantium, who was hoping thereby to thwart a papal crusade for the reestablishment of the Latin Empire. The Byzantine emperor was especially concerned about Charles of Anjou, who had his eye on the throne of Constantinople.

Charles, however, soon had to face a considerable distraction, which turned out to be the greatest challenge of his career. In 1282 trouble erupted in Sicily. An uprising against his rule, known as the Sicilian Vespers, overthrew his government and resulted in the loss of the island for the Angevins.

The Sicilians offered the crown to Peter III of Aragon, but Pope Martin IV (Simon de Brion) continued to support Charles, and proclaimed the dethronement of Peter III from his throne of Aragon for accepting the crown of Sicily. Martin IV commissioned Philip III of France to execute the sentence of deposition. The pope also offered the crown of Aragon to the French king, who accepted the dangerous prize for his third son, Charles of Valois. This papal juggling of the crowns of the world, however, proved to be futile because after a short war both kings died in 1285.

The papacy had become a great political institution, which found its embodiment in Boniface VIII Caetani, who ascended the papal throne in 1294, after inducing the aged hermit, Celestine V, to resign. "The throne of Peter was no place for a mystic" (Binns 1995, 55). Boniface was well aware that the papacy required at its helm a statesman. He was completely imbued by the pope's position as the head of the great confederacy of Europe and the source of a system of international law.

Shortly after his ascension Boniface VIII mediated the conflict between the houses of Anjou and Aragon by making territorial judgments. In 1297 he invested King James II of Aragon with Sardinia and Corsica. (In accordance with the papal grant, confirmed by Pope John XXII, the Aragonese, in 1323, began the conquest of Sardinia.) James II, in turn, had to agree to give up Sicily to Charles II. The Sicilians, however, did not meekly submit to this switch and invited Peter of Aragon's third son, Frederick, to be their king.

The Caetani pope had to face more reverses in his career. The papacy succeeded in destroying the power of the empire, but did not foresee a great new force, nationalism, which was to roll back, slowly but inexorably, the universal and supranational government of the pope.

Philip IV of France launched the first challenge by a national state to the universal monarchy of the papacy. Boniface's problems with Philip grew out of papal efforts to secure the peace in the conflict between England and France over Guienne and Flanders. Since both kings, Edward I and Philip IV, taxed their clergy to pay for the expenses of the war, the pope, as a means of stopping the hostilities, tried to cut off the funds. In 1296 he issued the bull *Clericos laicos*, which barred, under automatic excommunication, royal taxation of the church without papal license.

In England the papal bull was enforced, but Philip IV of France countered by prohibiting the export of gold and silver from France, thus cutting off the papal revenues. The position the pope took was well within the established tenets of canon law. The problem was that he did not perceive the changed circumstances and lacked all sense of diplomacy. Living in a mental world of his own, he did not grasp the fact that politics is the art of the possible, and could not read the signs of the times.

Another factor contributing to the feud was the character of Philip IV (the Fair) who, as later events proved, was completely lacking moral restraints in the choice of his means. One would never have guessed that he was the grandson of St. Louis. The French king and the pope had identical dreams: to concentrate all authority, political and spiritual, in their hands.

The financial problems were eventually reconciled, but a new crisis arose when the bishop of Pamiers was arrested in France. Faced with this new provocation, the pope summoned the king and threatened him with deposition. Boniface VIII attempted to enforce the universal authority of the papacy over all national governments as asserted by Gregory VII and maintained by Innocent III. He was determined to counter forcefully the usurpation of papal powers by the national monarchies as spearheaded by Philip IV, the Fair, of France.

The pope kept up the offensive. In 1302 he issued the bull *Unam sanctam*, in which he asserted that "the spiritual power must establish the temporal power and pass judgement on it" and that whoever resisted this papal power, "resisteth the ordinance of God" (Viorst 1965, 68). It was one of the strongest statements in support of the universal world monarchy of the papacy.

But the king of France marched to a different drumbeat. The concept of the sovereign nation clashed directly with the medieval theory of a universal and omnipotent Papal Commonwealth. Philip IV sent the French vice chancellor, Guillaume de Nogaret, to Italy to stir up a rebellion in the Papal States and to forestall the publication of a bull of excommunication and deposition against the French king.

With the help of the Colonna, archenemies of the Caetani, Nogaret succeeded in storming the papal palace in Anagni and capturing the pope. Although the local citizens eventually freed Boniface and chased the French away, the strain was too much for him and he died shortly thereafter.

With Boniface VIII fell the imperial papacy. The pope believed his power to be inviolable and permanent, but the French king has shown that it was nothing of the sort. The universal Papal Commonwealth had encountered a new force, the national state, that proved to be, in the long run, a more formidable opponent than the old empire had been.

The power of tradition and precedent, however, dies slowly, and while the conflict with Philip of France signaled the decline, it did not end the Papal Monarchy. What it clearly indicated was that formal legal pronouncements are worthless unless they can be enforced. This lesson is valid even today.

During the contest with France, Boniface VIII succeeded in detaching the German king, Albert of Habsburg, from his alliance with Philip IV by recognizing him, in 1303, as prospective emperor, after the king acknowledged the pope's right to bestow the crown.

Papal power over Germany remained secure as long as the German kings retained their ambition to wear the imperial diadem. During the Middle Ages, "none denied that it was by the Pope alone that the crown could be lawfully imposed" (Bryce 1889, 219).

> The pontiff asserted the transference of the Empire as a fief, and declared that the power of Peter, symbolized by the two keys, was temporal as well as spiritual (Bryce 1889, 209).

The emperor was, according to the papal theory of government, a lieutenant, the secular arm in the execution of the papal plan. This papal political theory was driven home in the imperial coronation rites. Medieval ceremonies always expressed a program clothed in symbols understandable to contemporaries. The reason the popes could turn the table on the emperors was a result of their legal and ideological preparedness.

Papal coronations, as opposed to imperial coronations, on the other hand, had no constitutional or sacral significance. The candidate became pope immediately upon his election. The coronation was performed only to show by contemporary and suitable means the pope's sovereign power. During the Middle Ages, the modern state system of Europe began to develop. Feudal lordships slowly coalesced and grew into nations. The Germanic Holy Roman Empire, in spite of its lofty claims, turned out to be just one of them. Only the papal organization retained its international and universal character and gave unity to the continent.

At the end of the Middle Ages, the pope still wielded immense administrative, financial, and judicial power throughout Europe. In the words of the Encyclopedia Britannica, the papacy in the Middle Ages "was the only highly developed and stable institution and as such gave the world, by virtue of its government, a sense of unity, order and purpose" (Encyc. Brit. 1963, s.v. "Papacy").

Renaissance and Reformation

In 1305, Bertrand de Got, a Frenchman, ascended the papal throne as Clement V. Four years later, he transferred his court to Avignon. Popes who successfully resolved disputes among the kings of Europe, and whose decrees made thrones shake and tumble in the four corners of the continent, were very often unable to control the bloody feuds on their own doorstep. This may be the political equivalent of the adage that familiarity breeds contempt.

At Avignon, on the rocks above the Rhone, next to the papal territory of Venaissin, the pope found a more congenial atmosphere. Avignon was at the time not a part of France, but a possession of the pope's vassal, the king of Naples and count of Provence.

Clement V was in many ways subservient to the king of France and even cooperated with him, though reluctantly, in one of the great judicial crimes in history, the destruction of Knights Templar. But he managed to show sometimes a streak of independence, and strongly maintained the papal claims to universal monarchy.

The French pope even stood up to Philip IV of France and refused to promote his brother, Charles of Valois, to the imperial throne, which would have enshrined French dominion over Europe. The pope, as a counterweight to French power, supported the candidacy of Henry of Luxemburg (Henry VII).

When the medieval universal Papal Commonwealth collapsed and a medley of national states arose from its ashes, establishing and maintaining a balance of powers became the chief focus of papal policy. For this reason the pope did not wish to see the same dynasty on the thrones of France and the Holy Roman Empire.

Clement V commissioned three cardinals to crown Henry VII in Rome in 1312, impressing on the world that, while he resided in Avignon, the imperial crown was still a gift of the papal throne. A year later, however, when Emperor Henry came into conflict with King Robert of Naples, the pope came to the aid of his vassal and threatened Henry with excommunication if he did not agree to an armistice.

On the death of the emperor, Clement published a bull maintaining that the oath taken by the king of the Romans to the pope was an oath of vassalage. Consequently, as suzerain of the empire, he took over the administration during the vacancy and appointed King Robert of Naples imperial vicar in Italy.

With the contested election of 1314 between Louis Wittelsbach of Bavaria and Frederick Habsburg of Austria, however, a new crisis was brewing in the empire. Pope John XXII (Jacques Duèse) decided to continue the policy of Clement V and to keep the imperial throne vacant until he decided on the right candidate. At the same time he maintained Robert of Naples as imperial vicar in Italy.

Echoing his predecessor, John XXII asserted that during an interregnum the power of the emperor devolves on the pope "to whom God had assigned power on earth." (Gontard 1964, 318.) He also reminded the world "that the right of the German Electors to choose a king of the Romans came expressly from the pope, who must first examine and approve him" (Gontard 1964, 319).

When Louis of Bavaria defeated his opponent in 1322 and began to act as the rightful ruler, the pope declared him guilty of assuming the title of king of the Romans without papal confirmation, and threatened him with the ban of the church. Thus, the stage was set for the last great contest in the empire between the Guelfs (the papal party) and the Ghibellines (the imperial party).

Marsiglio of Padua and William of Occam took up the cause of Louis against the pope, foreshadowing the future separation of church and state. They maintained that since Christ did not exercise, nor claim, temporal power during his life on earth, He could not have delegated such powers to his vicar.

These ideas were also espoused by the German electors, who declared at Rense in 1338 that their election confers on the candidate the imperial throne, without the need for papal confirmation. The declaration was given legal form in the law *Licet Juris* at the diet at Frankfurt in the same year. These steps were clear reactions to the use of ecclesiastical censures for political purposes.

This line of reasoning was, of course, banned by the pope, and implementation of such theories was still far in the future. Papal power remained paramount and the German kings who followed Louis continued to seek papal approbation.

Finally, Louis himself saw the need to free himself of the papal ban and was willing to make humiliating concessions, but they were not enough to appease the angry passions of the pope. On the 13th of April 1346, Clement VI (Pierre Roger de Beaufort) pronounced Louis deposed, and on the 11th of July Charles of Luxemburg, king of Bohemia, in open alliance with the pope, was elected German king at Rense. After the dethronement of Louis IV, Charles IV "received the gift or promise of the vacant empire from the Roman pontiffs, who, in the exile and captivity of Avignon, affected the dominion of the earth" (Gibbon 1960, 646).

Louis died a year later, and the pope's hand-picked candidate became the undisputed master of Germany. Charles IV committed himself to respect the territorial integrity of the Papal States, and not to enter Italy without the permission of the pope. He was crowned emperor in Rome by the cardinal bishop of Ostia on Easter Sunday 1355.

The following year Charles issued the Golden Bull which restricted the number of imperial electors to seven: three ecclesiastical and four lay princes. They were the same seven electors confirmed by two papal bulls issued by Pope Urban IV a century earlier (in 1263). Although the Golden Bull remained silent on the need for papal confirmation, traditions die slowly. After the election of Rupert in 1400, the electors immediately requested papal approval from Boniface IX. The emperors following Rupert, Sigismund and Frederick III, both sought papal approbation.

The pope's struggle with Louis IV undoubtedly inflicted some injury on the papacy, and to some it may even have appeared a Pyrrhic victory. In the end, however, papal power had been vindicated and gave the pope a sense of supremacy over the state system of Europe. The old world order was still intact, and a papal ban still proved to be a weapon that could mortally cripple an adversary.

Meanwhile, in 1348, Pope Clement VI acquired Avignon by purchase from Queen Joanna of Naples and countess of Provence. Now the pope stood on his own soil. He incorporated the city into the neighboring Comtat Venaissin, which had been a papal possession since 1218, when Raymond VII, count of Toulouse, ceded it to Pope Honorius III (confirmed to Gregory X by King Philip III of France in 1274). The territory remained under papal sovereignty, garrisoned by papal forces, until annexed to France by the revolutionary government in 1791.

In time, the popes realized that a return to Rome, which still held the glamour and traditions of the mistress of the world, would entail certain advantages, especially since Avignon no longer provided the required security. When a motley army converged on Avignon, Innocent VI (Etienne Aubert) found it necessary to increase the fortifications in the city.

The pope dispatched the vigorous and aggressive Cardinal Egidio de Albornoz, former archbishop of Toledo and chancellor of Castile, to reestablish papal authority in the Roman States. As commander of the papal armies, Albornoz succeeded in reducing the pontifical territories to obedience. Urban V (Guillaume Grimoard) was the first Avignonese pope to return to Rome, which under his successors again became the seat of the papal government.

At the same time, in the east, the pressure on Byzantium mounted. In 1369 Urban V was visited in Rome by John V Paleologus, asking for help against the Turks, recalling earlier appeals from Constantinople to the papal throne. The Byzantine emperor, to gain the pope's favor, accepted the full authority of the Holy See in his domains in a ceremony on the steps of St. Peter's. The Orthodox clergy, however, never recognized this act.

Urban's successor, Gregory XI (another Pierre Roger de Beaufort, nephew of Clement VI), in an effort to pacify Italy, unleashed the papal armies, under the command of Amadeus VI of Savoy, against the Visconti in Milan, and, under the command of Cardinal Robert of Geneva, against rebel cities in Italy. The pope also laid an interdict on Florence, voiding her trade agreements and blocking her markets, thus completely paralyzing her banking and commercial life.

These tribulations of Italy were only the beginning chapters of more extensive disturbances in Europe. Under Urban VI (Bartolomeo Prignano) the Great Schism began. His election in 1378 may have upset the balance of his mind. He was judged deranged by the French cardinals, who deposed him and elected Robert of Geneva as the antipope "Clement VII." Clement was the son of the count of Geneva and was also related to the king of France. From then on a pope sat at Rome, and another at Avignon.

The division of Europe followed the dictates of political expediency. France, Burgundy, Savoy, Naples, Scotland, Castile and Aragon acknowledged Clement, while Germany, England, the north Italian states, Hungary and Poland held out for Urban. Urban VI deposed Queen Joanna of Naples because she was sympathetic to the pope of Avignon, and arranged a marriage between Richard II of England and Anne of Bohemia to retain the allegiance of Bohemia. (Binns 1995, 159.)

The Great Schism continued into the 15th century. The Council of Constance, by deposing the antipopes "John XXIII" and "Benedict XIII" and receiving the abdication of Gregory XII, finally ended the division. The cardinals elected Oddo Colonna, who took the name of Martin V, and immediately began to consolidate his power. At his coronation the future Emperor Sigismund and Frederick of Brandenburg held the reins of his steed. The pope defeated the condottiere Braccione di Montone at L'Aquila in 1424, crushed the revolt by Bologna in 1429, and reestablished papal authority in the Roman States.

Martin's successor, Pope Eugenius IV (Gabriele Condulmaro), in 1433, crowned king Sigismund emperor at Rome. Five years later Eugenius presided over the Council of Florence, which was a triumph of papal diplomacy; it put the seal on the defeat of the conciliar movement, which tried to limit the authority of the pope. Eugenius exploited, in a statesmanlike manner, all opportunities and reclaimed a large measure of the pope's traditional powers and privileges.

At Florence, John VII Paleologus, forced by the imminent danger of a Turkish invasion, agreed to a union of the Byzantine church with Rome under the supremacy of the pope, but, as earlier, it proved ephemeral. The Byzantine emperor new that only a massive new crusade from the west could save his empire, and directed a last desperate plea for help to the pope. Eugenius IV did, indeed, organize a large campaign, led by King Wladislaus (Ulaszlo) of Hungary, against the Ottoman Empire, but it ended in a disaster at Varna in 1443.

The Middle Ages were slowly drawing to a close. The coronation of Frederick III by Pope Nicholas V (Tommaso Parentucelli) was the last such act performed in Rome with the traditional ceremony. First, on the 16th of March, the pope officiated at the marriage of Frederick III and Leonora of Portugal. During the proceedings "some of the Cardinals had precedence over Frederick, who as yet only ranked as German king" (Creighton 1897, 3:124).

Three days later, on the 19th of March, the imperial investiture took place with due pomp and ceremony. Frederick took the oath of obedience to the pope and, after the coronation, when Nicholas mounted his steed, the emperor held the reins of his horse for a few paces. Thus, the coronation in 1452 clearly brought out for the last time, in all its symbolism, the proper relationship between the two powers.

Meanwhile, in the east, the Byzantine Empire was tottering. Constantinople fell to Mohammed the Conqueror in 1453. The pope again placed himself at the head of the European commonwealth, and proclaimed another crusade to liberate the capital of the East. Great plans were made, but in the end they all fizzled out. For a moment the fall of Constantinople brought back the medieval dream of a crusade, but it soon became evident that by the second half of the 15th century the fiery enthusiasm for holy wars was a thing of the past.

In 1458 Pius II (Enea Silvio Piccolomini), a well known humanist and writer, ascended the chair of Peter. A typical product of the Renaissance, he advised the emperor that it was vain for a prince to please the people, because the multitude was always fickle, and it is dangerous to let them have their way. Democracy was definitely not in style in the 15th century.

In the kingdom of Naples, Pius reversed the policy of his predecessor, Calixtus III (Alfonso de Borja), and recognized Ferdinand I instead of the French candidate, René I of Anjou, creating thereby some diplomatic problems with France. He, too, planned to lead a crusade in person for the recovery of Constantinople, but died in

Ancona, in 1464, on the eve of the enterprise.

The presiding position of the pope over the European state system was still unchallenged in the 15th century. Frederick III on a visit to Rome in 1469 tried to obtain from Pope Paul II (Pietro Barbo) recognition of his claims to the thrones of Bohemia and Hungary and for his planned transfer of the electoral dignity from Bohemia to Austria. Pope Paul, who in 1466 deposed George Podiebrad from the throne of Bohemia, however, put his hopes on Matthias of Hungary, who had already proved his unquestioned loyalty to the papal throne. The pope had no wish to alienate such an important champion.

As the spirit of the Renaissance began to permeate the intellectual climate of Europe, people slowly discarded the medieval preoccupation with otherworldly pursuits and embraced the pleasures and accomplishments of this world. This change in outlook was also reflected in the papacy. In fact, some of the popes became leading figures of the Renaissance.

In the new humanistic atmosphere the popes also rediscovered women. Many pontiffs of this period sacrificed their reputations on the altar of the goddess of love. They acknowledged and legitimized their children, bestowed on them duchies and principalities, and married them into the ruling houses of Europe. In fact, papal policy was often determined by these, sometimes brittle, alliances.

Pope Sixtus IV (Francesco della Rovere), who ruled from 1471 to 1484, was a good example of a Renaissance prince. His nephew Leonardo della Rovere married a daughter of the king of Naples, and another nephew Giovanni della Rovere married the daughter of the last Montefeltro duke of Urbino, and was designated by the pope as the successor to the duchy.

The pope's interferences in Florence, Venice, Milan, and Naples detracted from the prestige of the papal throne and reduced him to a petty Italian despot. His only contribution to the defense of the European commonwealth was the fleet he equipped for a naval campaign against the Ottoman Empire. In spite of that effort, the Turks succeeded in taking Otranto and holding it for a short time.

Innocent VIII (Giovanni Battista Cibo) who succeeded to the papal throne in 1484 was also a typical representative of the Renaissance. He was the first pope to recognize his children. The marriage of his son, Franceschetto Cibo, to a daughter of Lorenzo de Medici was the cause for bestowing the cardinal's hat on her brother Giovanni, the future Leo X. Innocent's granddaughter was married to a grandson of King

Ferdinand I (Ferrante) of Naples, although the pope's relationship with the king was not always smooth.

Innocent VIII was also the first pope to enter into relations with the Ottoman sultans. Prince Djem, who was defeated by his brother Bayezid II, fled to the Knights of St. John, who eventually handed him over to the pope. Innocent made an arrangement with the sultan, and for a yearly fee of 40,000 ducats kept Djem a prisoner in Rome to keep him from contesting the Ottoman throne.

The second Borgia pope, Alexander VI, was perhaps the best known pontiff of the high Renaissance. He was unscrupulous and sensuous, but, in spite of his lax morals, never neglected the duties of his office. His bearing was dignified and charming, and he had "an amazing gift for exciting the affections of women" (Tuchman 1984, 76).

Alexander was 59 when, still succumbing to the temptations of the flesh, he took the beautiful 19 year old Gulia Farnese, with flowing golden hair, as his mistress. Thus started the rise of the house of Farnese. Alexander was so impressed by her that he raised her brother to the purple. He eventually became Pope Paul III, who established his house in Parma, and through Elizabeth Farnese became an ancestor of the royal house of Spain.

Alexander VI married his eldest son Juan, duke of Gandia, to a Spanish princess and enfeoffed him in 1497 with the duchy of Benevento. He even entertained the idea of raising him to the throne of Naples. But the pope's relations with King Ferdinand I improved after the marriage of one of his other sons, Jofre, to the king's granddaughter. As a result Alexander supported Ferdinand against the claims of Charles VIII of France to the throne of Naples.

After King Ferdinand's death, the pope recognized and crowned his son Alfonso II king of Naples. Thereupon the French king appeared in Rome in 1494, at the head of his army, to enforce his demands on a reluctant pope. He was bent on obtaining his investiture with the kingdom of Naples and his appointment as the leader of a crusade against the Turks. In spite of his show of force, Charles VIII was determined to avoid provoking the open hostility of Alexander for fear of intervention from Germany and Spain.

The pope, however, did not take any chances and sought refuge in the Castle Sant'Angelo, which he connected by secret passage to the Vatican. Then he dispatched a commission to berate the king about the reaction of other princes when they see that he besieged the pope "and claims to judge him, to whom God has committed the judgment of all men" (Creighton 1897, 4:232).

Alexander's diplomacy produced some results. In January 1495 the Borgia pope had the satisfaction of receiving from Charles VIII the obedience of France. In an official audience the king kissed the pope's foot and hand, and recited the brief formula: "Holy Father, I have come to swear obedience and reverence to Your Holiness in the manner of my predecessors, the kings of France" (Cloulas 1987, 111).

In spite of Charles' submission, Pope Alexander still refused his request for the investiture of Naples. Under the new French king, Louis XII, Alexander VI maintained good relations with France, annulled the king's current marriage and gave him dispensation to marry Anne of Brittany. The king, in turn, provided the pope's son, Cesare Borgia, with a princess of Navarre and made him duke of Valentinois. Relations improved so much that in 1501 Alexander VI partitioned the kingdom of Naples between France and Spain.

During the feudal period, the Papal States shared the fate of the rest of Europe. Lands had been assigned to vassals over whom the central authority exercised only limited control. Alexander tried to reduce these vassals and to impose direct papal rule over the States of the Church. He appointed his son, Cesare, commander-in-chief of the papal army and started a systematic war to reduce the powerful barons of central Italy.

This policy was in line with general developments in Europe, where the loose feudal ties gave way to a centralized government and the modern states of France, Spain, and England came into being. The great fiefs were absorbed, and the kings evolved from overlords with vassals into sovereigns with subjects.

In addition, the pope named Cesare duke of the Romagna and dreamed of reducing Italy to a Borgia domain. The other powers of the peninsula trembled at the prospect of a powerful central Italian state, which was backed by the worldwide authority of the papacy, and viewed the progress of papal arms with alarm. Cesare Borgia, the model of Machiavelli's *Prince*, was an able administrator, but had a rather sinister reputation even in an age renowned for cruelty, treachery, cynicism, and greed.

Alexander VI's most lasting achievement, however, was the settlement of the conflicting colonial claims of Spain and Portugal as a result of Columbus' discoveries. As so often in the past, the pope again acted in his capacity as global monarch. In 1493, by the bull *Inter caetera*, Alexander Borgia divided the globe between the two powers.

He assigned America to Spain and Africa and Asia to Portugal, assuring peace among the colonial nations for a century.

The popes were always aware of the importance of military might in the pursuit of their global mission. Julius II, the second Rovere pope, realized that in order to assure a free, powerful, and independent papacy, he must make the Papal States the dominant and strongest military power on the Italian peninsula. He viewed this as essential to keep other European powers at bay, and to enable the papacy to maintain its worldwide leadership.

Considered the refounder of the Papal States, Julius II, in full armor and sword in hand, conquered Perugia and Bologna in 1506, laid an interdict on Venice and defeated her through an alliance with France, Germany and Spain, forcing her to give up Rimini and Faenza. The pope was not choosy in his means. As he said, "When I get no help from St. Peter's keys, I must get help from his sword" (Gontard 1964, 361). Julius II realized that "virtue without power" would make the pope "a mere slave of Kings" (Tuchman 1984, 103).

Then, when the power of France became too overbearing the pope formed an alliance with Venice and Spain against her. Julius II started the papacy's reliance on Swiss mercenaries, which gave him a fighting edge in the Italian wars. In 1510 he enfeoffed Ferdinand II of Aragon with the kingdom of Naples, disregarding the claims of the French king. By 1512 the French were forced to leave Italy, and the pope succeeded in adding Parma, Piacenza and Emilia to the Papal States. Julius II again made the papacy the center around which the politics of Europe revolved.

In 1508, when Venice refused passage to the German king Maximilian on his way to Rome for his imperial coronation, Julius II issued a bull granting him the style of "emperor- elect," which remained the formal title of German kings until the end of the Holy Roman Empire in 1806.

Pope Julius II was succeeded by Leo X, second son of Lorenzo de Medici. Easy going, but devious and scheming, he appreciated the pleasures of life, and greeted his elevation with the exclamation, "Let us enjoy the papacy, now that God has given it to us." He induced Francis I of France to abolish the Pragmatic Sanction of Bourges, enacted in 1438 to limit papal powers in the country, and in 1513 he received the submission of France (Creighton 1897, 4: 217).

His vacillating stance in the matter of the imperial succession betrayed his Medici mentality. Both of the major candidates, Charles I of Spain and Francis I of France, made attempts to bribe the pope, whose stand was deemed critical. Francis prodded the pope to stand up to Charles and "be Leo in deed as well as in name" (Creighton 1897, 4:110), but Leo played the game with Medicean duplicity. He knew that whether the king of Spain or the king of France gained the empire, the balance of powers in Europe would be upset with grave consequences for the papacy.

Pope Leo X toyed with the idea of promoting the cause of Frederick, duke of Saxony, for the throne. A weak emperor in constant need of papal support would have retained for the sovereign pontiff the position of arbiter of kings, and would have maintained the balance of powers in Europe. Leo also explored the possibility of the candidacy of Henry VIII of England. Cardinal Wolsey, however, was not willing to embrace this step without a firm commitment of the pope to the English cause.

No one really knew what Leo's policy was if, indeed, he had one. But we know that he was a believer in *Realpolitik*: "Having made a treaty with one party," he said, " there is no reason why one should not treat with the other" (Tuchman 1984, 108).

Finally, under pressure of events, a deal was struck. Leo X gave permission to Charles to hold Naples together with the empire, setting aside an earlier bull prohibiting it. Charles, in turn, agreed to pay a yearly tribute of 8000 ducats to the papal treasury and to maintain two galleys for the defense of papal territories. Cajetan, the papal legate in Germany, was instructed to inform the electors that the pope removed all bar to Charles' election.

In reality the pope's vacillations and intrigues resulted in his loss of control over the proceedings. He frankly confessed to the envoy of the Republic of Venice that "it was no use to knock his head against the wall" (Creighton 1897, 4:117).

It was under Leo X that Martin Luther, in protest against the sale of indulgences, lighted the torch of the Reformation. Ironically it came at a time when the papacy had reestablished its historic dignity and had firmly rooted its political power in Italy. Leo at first dismissed the affair as "squabbling monks," but eventually had to face reality. The Reformation turned out to be the greatest blow to the papacy's political and ideological might.

In 16th century Italy, the otherwise cynical Machiavelli could still assert (in Chapter XI of *The Prince*) that only ecclesiastical states are secure and happy because they are "exalted and maintained by God."

Judging by the spread of the Reformation, however, quite a number of people north of the Alps could no longer accept the thesis that the dynastic schemes, martial endeavors, and financial policies of the Borgia, Rovere, and Medici popes were exalted and maintained by God. During the Renaissance, the popes began to lose that moral authority that was the foundation of their power.

The emperor, true to his historic mission, joined the pope in his attempts to check the Lutheran revolt and to maintain the unity of the European commonwealth. Leo X excommunicated Luther in 1521, and Charles V placed him under the ban of the empire in the same year. These steps, however, did not end the revolt against the papacy, but rather started 150 years of slaughter and devastation.

Clement VII (Giulio de Medici), who ascended the papal throne in 1523, was cultivated and hard working, but followed the shifty policy of his cousin, Leo X. When Clement, after several flip-flopping alliances, joined the league of Cognac against the growing power of Charles V, who ruled both Germany and Spain, the imperial army moved into Italy.

Charles, who had a profound respect for the papacy, was reluctant to order a strike against the Holy See, but the undisciplined and underpaid German and Spanish mercenaries under the command of the Constable of Bourbon mutinied and in 1527 sacked the city.

Rome was at the mercy, not of a conquering army, but of a host of demons inspired only by avarice, cruelty, and lust .... the groans of the dying were only interrupted by the blasphemies of the soldiers, and the shrieks of agonizing women who were being violated or hurled out of the windows (Creighton 1897, 4:342).

Now at last Clement VII began to understand the magnitude of the catastrophe that he brought upon himself. The Swiss Guards fell almost to the last man in defense of the pope who was besieged in the Castle Sant'Angelo. The terrible *sacco di Roma* put an end to the greatness of Rome in this epoch and brought an abrupt end to the period of the high Renaissance.

This calamity was preceded by another blow. On the 30th of August 1526, on the plains of Mohacs, the king of Hungary, Louis II, perished with his whole army, and Sultan Suleiman had the road free to the heart of Europe.

Suddenly Clement VII realized with a shock that his political intrigues in Europe were not in keeping with his traditional mission of protecting the European commonwealth. He therefore renewed his pleas for peace and for common action against the Ottoman Empire. His precarious relationship with the emperor-elect Charles V was, however, not very conducive for a campaign against the Turks.

Eventually both potentates realized that they needed each other. The reconciliation between Clement VII and Charles V was clinched by a deal: The pope crowned Charles emperor in Bologna in 1530 (the last coronation of a Holy Roman emperor by a pope) and invested him with the kingdom of Naples; the emperor, in turn, used his troops to restore Clement's family, the Medici, to power in Florence.

In spite of this reconciliation, Pope Clement VII remained conscious of the need to counterbalance the power of Charles and made a rapprochement with France. He was present at Marseilles in 1533 to marry his grandniece, Catarina de Medici, to the second son of Francis I, the future King Henry II. It was here that he authorized the French expedition to North America, circumventing the assignment of the continent to Spain by the bulls of Pope Alexander VI.

Clement's relationship with England, however, did not have such a happy ending. In the 16th century a crisis of far-reaching consequences developed between the papacy and the king of England. Earlier Pope Julius II had good relations with Henry VIII, granting him dispensation in 1503 to marry his brother's widow, Catharine of Aragon. Although the king defended the papal authority against Luther in 1521, for which he received from Pope Leo X the title of "Defender of the Faith," the relationship soured when he wanted to divorce his wife, so that he could marry Anne Boleyn.

The situation got somewhat complicated in 1529, when Pope Clement VII made a compact of reconciliation with Charles V who was, rather inconveniently, the nephew of Catharine of Aragon. In view of this relationship, Clement was hesitant to grant the English king's request. When Henry broke with his wife and married Anne Boleyn in 1533, the pope excommunicated the king and declared his divorce and remarriage void. As a result, Henry VIII founded the Church of England, which was for the papacy a greater disaster than the revolt in Germany.

The popes finally realized the need for constructive efforts to stem the tide of revolt. Paul III (Alessandro Farnese) was the pope who granted the charter to the Society of Jesus, which spearheaded the Counter-Reformation. The Jesuits were destined to acquire great political power and were feared by national governments because of their special vow of obedience to the pope.

In spite of these efforts, Paul III was still inspired by the spirit of the late Renaissance. He favored artists and writers, and enjoyed masked balls and sumptuous feasts. In 1545 he carved Parma and Piacenza out of the Papal States and bestowed it as an independent duchy on his son Pierluigi Farnese.

Although in the 16th century popes still ratified treaties among nations and maintained a certain position of primacy among the kings of the world, developments in Germany, England, and France provided many signs that a new age was dawning. From then on, the papacy fought a rearguard action.

Pope Pius V (Michele Ghislieri), who ascended to the chair of Peter in 1566, did not meekly submit to the loss of England. Under Elizabeth I he stirred up a rebellion in the north of the country and, in 1570, issued the bull *Regnan in excelsis*, depriving "Elizabeth of her pretended claim to the kingdom." After the northern revolt was crushed, however, Englishmen were allowed to remain loyal to the queen until such time that the bull of deposition could be put into effect.

Both France and Spain considered the papal action against Elizabeth justified and made plans for enforcing it. The papacy also took steps to implement its judgment. Under Gregory XIII (Ugo Boncompagni) a papal army was outfitted under Thomas Stukeley for the invasion of Ireland, but was eventually diverted for a crusade in Morocco.

It was under Pope Sixtus V (Felice Peretti-Montalto), who succeeded Gregory, that the crisis over England came to a head. Earlier the duke of Guise had plans to invade England from France, but in the end only Philip II of Spain heeded the pope's call to execute the sentence of deposition against Queen Elizabeth.

Sixtus earmarked huge subsidies for the naval expedition, and "retained for himself the disposition of the crown" (Gontard 1964, 444). In the end, the destruction of the Spanish Armada in the English Channel in 1588 saved the throne of the Virgin Queen. This was the last instance that the papacy used this, by now ineffective and outdated, form of censure against a ruling sovereign.

A few years earlier, in 1562, the Reformation also spread to France and ignited a series of religious wars. Pope Pius V gave military and financial support to Catarina de Medici against the Huguenots. His greatest achievement, however, was the Holy League he brought about against the Ottoman Empire. The combined Spanish, Venetian, and papal fleet, consisting of 200 galleons, inflicted a crushing defeat on the Turkish navy at Lepanto in 1571, shattering its power in the Mediterranean.

Pius' successor, Pope Gregory XIII, also supported the Catholic League in France, but he is best known for ordering the reform of the calendar, which involved the dropping of 10 days (5-14 October 1582) and the establishment of leap years, to bring it in line with the seasons. The Gregorian calendar took immediate effect in Catholic countries, and was in time accepted throughout the world.

Meanwhile, the war in France continued. In 1585 Pope Sixtus V pronounced the excommunication of Henry of Navarre, the leader of the Huguenot forces. Gregory XIV (Niccolo Sfondrati) renewed the ban on Henry and dispatched a papal army to France. His successor, Innocent IX (Gian Antonio Fachinetti), also supported the Catholic League and attempted with the papal army to raise the siege of Rouen.

It was under the Aldobrandini Pope, Clement VIII, that the French wars of religion finally came to an end. Henry of Navarre, in a shrewd political move, abjured Protestantism, and with the motto "Paris is worth a mass" embraced the Catholic faith. In 1595 Clement VIII, after public penance of Henry's ambassadors in Rome, lifted the ban and recognized him as the rightful king of France. Secretly, Clement even welcomed the opportunity to reestablish the balance of powers in Europe by building up Henry IV against the overbearing power of Philip II of Spain.

With the 16th century ended the Italian Renaissance. The pope had to adjust his policies, as he moved from dominance to leadership during the early modern period. During the high Middle Ages he could impose his decrees on the most powerful sovereigns. With the changing political environment during the Renaissance, he had to consistently try to maintain the balance of powers and adjust his support accordingly.

Only when the forces among rulers were evenly matched, could the pope, by throwing his support to one or the other, effectively assert his leadership. He had to prevent the accumulation of marginal geopolitical gains by any country, which over time would change the political equilibrium. In pursuing their policies, the popes had to adjust their moral idealism to the way the world actually worked.

During the Renaissance the modern concept of the state began to replace the church as the guiding social reality. The 15th and 16th century popes were princes of the Renaissance, for the most part creating duchies and principalities for their families, making and breaking treaties, conducting petty wars, and throwing themselves into the intricate and corrupt game of Italian power politics.

Over time, the pope was reduced from his exalted position of a world monarch to a mere equal of the other sovereigns. Rulers stirred by growing national consciousness resented the payment of taxes to a pope whom they merely regarded as an Italian potentate, and the appeal of cases from their national courts to the papal court at Rome.

As long as the papal policy was favorable to their goals, the kings of Europe raised no objections to the exalted claims of the papacy, which enabled the popes to recoup their positions after so many stumblings. The papal throne was so intimately identified as the hub around which world politics revolved, that every king who could command some advantage from it was only too glad to uphold it.

The streamlining of papal finances, began by the Avignonese popes (who had to compensate for the loss of revenue from the Papal States), drained large sums of money from all countries of Europe, and began to generate resentment by the national monarchies. The laxity of morals at the papal court during the Renaissance also created disillusionment in a large segment of the population. As the pope's political and moral leadership declined, national monarchs started to take steps to limit papal judicial and administrative authority.

During the 16th century the medieval ideal of a Europe united under the papal banner became unraveled. Papal hegemony was no longer palatable to many of the rulers of the continent, and the position of the Papal Monarchy as an institution of universal scope and validity was beginning to be called into question.

The New Secular World Order

At the beginning of the 17th century, Paul V (Camillo Borghese) still insisted on the somewhat outdated medieval powers of the papacy. He imposed ecclesiastical censures on Naples and Venice that were later resolved by compromise. By this time in history, the secular governments considered the wording of papal bulls as nothing more than bombast and rhetoric. It slowly dawned on the papacy that interdicts were losing their effectiveness against post-medieval states. It was the last time that they were employed.

The Borghese pope had to face another conflict, when the English parliament passed an act requiring Catholics to deny under oath the pope's right to deprive sovereigns of their thrones. Paul V denounced the edict and forbade compliance.

A similar conflict arose in France when the Estates-General declared in 1614 that the king held his crown from God alone (not from the pope). In this case Paul V succeeded in forcing the withdrawal of this claim and obtained the dismissal of the dean of the Sorbonne, who supported the declaration. This foreshadowed the great feud later in the century between Louis XIV and Innocent XI.

The reign of Paul V also saw the start of the last great religious conflict, the Thirty-Years War (1618-1648), which left Germany starving, depopulated and in ruins. From 1620 on the pope granted subsidies to the Emperor Ferdinand II and the Catholic League.

Pope Gregory XV (Alessandro Ludovisi) also provided large subsidies to the emperor for the war in Germany, and also to the king of Poland for the war against the Ottoman Empire. He ensured that the electorate of the Palatinate of the Rhine, vacated by Frederick V, was transferred in 1623 to Maximilian of Bavaria, thus retaining a majority of Catholic electors in the empire.

It is one of the ironies of history that France under Cardinal Richelieu joined the Thirty Years War on the Protestant side. During the last phase of the conflict dynastic interests came to dominate the political constellations. On learning of the cardinal's death, Pope Urban VIII Barberini is believed to have commented, "If there is a God, the Cardinal de Richelieu will have much to answer for. If not ... well, he had a successful life" (Auchincloss 1972, 256).

With the peace of Westphalia, which finally ended the hostilities, the Protestant states in the empire

> were declared free from all jurisdiction of the Pope.... Thus the last link which bound Germany to Rome was snapped, the last of the principles by virtue of which the Empire had existed was abandoned.... The Peace of Westphalia was therefore an abrogation of the sovereignty of Rome (Bryce 1889, 343).

The Pamfili pope, Innocent X, certainly saw it that way and commanded his legate to protest against it. In the bull *Zelo domus Dei* of 1648 he declared the treaty null and void. By that time, however, the pope no longer had the capacity to shape world events. It was another example of a sweeping pronouncement without the ability to enforce it that is so damaging to the credibility of any authority.

The conflict with France over the Gallican liberties, which attempted to restrict papal powers, began under Alexander VII (Fabio Chigi) and continued under Innocent XI (Benedetto Odescalchi). In 1682 Louis XIV issued a declaration asserting that sovereigns

> cannot be deposed either directly or indirectly by the authority of the heads of the church; that their subjects cannot be granted dispensation to refuse the allegiance and obedience which they owe (Translations 1902, 4:26).

Although toward the end of the 17th century such a papal policy would have been beyond the scope of the age, the declaration shows that the awesome medieval powers of the papacy still occupied the mind of the most powerful of monarchs.

Innocent XI defied the French king, but the main thrust of his policy was the halting of the Turkish onslaught on the West. The pope's greatest achievement was the coalition he created against the Ottoman Empire, whose armies were advancing on Vienna in the heart of Europe. First, Innocent brought about an alliance between King John III (Sobieski) of Poland and the Emperor Leopold I, which saved the imperial city.

To keep the momentum going, the pope then he formed the Holy League of 1684 -- consisting of Austria, Poland, and Venice -- whose forces liberated Hungary and large areas of eastern Europe and ended the Turkish threat to the continent. This was perhaps the last time that the papacy decisively intervened on the international scene.

Relations with France improved under Innocent XII (Antonio Pignatelli). The king revoked the Gallican articles because he needed papal support for the Bourbon claim to the Spanish succession. In 1700 the childless Charles II of Spain, on his deathbed, "consulted the Pope and obtained his approval" (Ogg 1960, 257) to bequeath his realm to Philip, duke of Anjou, grandson of Louis XIV.

Meanwhile, feudal relationships between countries were slowly phased out. In 1713 the Treaty of Utrecht, without consulting the pope, disposed of the papal fiefs of Naples, Sicily, Sardinia, and Parma, making clear that papal suzerainty was no longer meaningful in the new world order. In spite of these developments, Innocent XIII (Michelangelo de Conti), having a conciliatory temperament, invested the Emperor Charles VI with Naples and Sicily. He also recognized the Old Pretender, "Charles III," as the rightful king of England and Scotland and paid him a subsidy.

Political arrangements in Italy, however, never had much permanence. In 1734 Don Carlos marched with the Spanish army through the Papal States and conquered Naples and Sicily. To win over Clement XII (Lorenzo Corsini) he named the pope's nephew, Bartolomeo Corsini, viceroy in the kingdom. The pope was pressured to "invest" Don Carlos as King Charles III, the first Bourbon king of Naples. The 18th century did not leave much room for an independent papal policy.

Under Clement XIII (Carlo della Torre Rezzonico), the Bourbon monarchies began their agitation against the political power of the Jesuits. In the 16th and 17th centuries the society, with its military discipline and unconditional obedience to the pope, was viewed by many monarchs as a threat to their authority.

A number of governments demanded their suppression, and even took military action: France occupied Avignon and Venaissin, and the Neapolitans overran the papal enclaves of Benevento and Pontecorvo. Clement XIV (Lorenzo Ganganelli) finally succumbed to the pressure and in 1773, in the interest of peace, dissolved the order. (The society was reestablished on general demand in 1814.)

The old world was slowly disappearing. Even within the pontifical domain, feudalism was coming to an end. The duchies and principalities of the papal families became an integral part of the central administration. The celebrated papal and princely families of the epoch -- Borghese, Aldobrandini, Ludovisi, Barberini, Pamfili, Odescalchi -- built themselves palaces, fountains, and villas and gave Rome its baroque appearance. The papal curia with its administrators, financial experts, military might, and host of accredited diplomats fitted in entirely with the absolutist courts of Europe.

During the course of history, a number of papal families also ruled, or contended for the thrones, in other European countries. The Visconti ruled over Milan. The French King Louis XII claimed the duchy of Milan through his ancestress Valentina Visconti, who married Louis of Orleans in 1387.

The Medici ruled over Florence. In 1570 Pope Pius V granted Cosimo de Medici the title of grand duke of Tuscany. Catarina de Medici and Marie de Medici became queens of France, and were regents for their sons Charles IX and Louis XIII, respectively.

ORSINI
Celestine III
Nicholas III
Benedict XIII

BARBERINI
Urban VIII

CONTI
Innocent III, Gregory IX
Alexander IV
Innocent XIII

CAETANI
Boniface VIII

BONCAMPAGNI
Gregory XIII

BORGHESE
Paul V

COLONNA
Martin V

VISCONTI
Gregory X

Figure 2.3: Selected Papal Coats of Arms

BORGIA
Calixtus III
Alexander VI

SAVELLI
Honorius III
Honorius IV

ALDOBRANDINI
Clement VIII

ROVERE
Sixtus IV
Julius II

MEDICI
Leo X, Clement VII
Pius IV, Leo XI

FARNESE
Paul III

PICCOLOMINI
Pius II
Pius III

ODESCALCHI
Innocent XI

Figure 2.3: Selected Papal Coats of Arms (Cont.)

The Farnese ruled the independent duchy of Parma and Piacenza, which Pope Paul III created for his son Pierluigi. After expiration of the male line, Elizabeth Farnese, who as the wife of Philip V was queen of Spain, secured the duchy for her son Philip de Bourbon.

Pope Urban VI toyed with the idea of installing his nephew, Francesco Prignano, on the throne of Naples. He was not the only pope who entertained ideas about establishing a dynasty in the southern kingdom. Pope Calixtus III also had seriously considered a plan to acquire the throne of Naples for Pedro Luis de Borgia; so did Alexander VI for his son Juan de Borgia.

Even the Medici had designs on the Neapolitan kingdom. Pope Leo X was scheming to secure the throne of Naples for Giuliano de Medici. He also had plans to obtain the duchy of Milan for Lorenzo de Medici. (Creighton 1897, 5:227.) And Livio Odescalchi, nephew of Pope Innocent XI, was a candidate for the throne of Poland, and in 1697 received a large block of votes in the Sejm.

In the 18th century the world was changing fast. With the French revolution, much of the old order was swept away. The presiding position of the pope over an international system was no longer considered relevant to the life of nations.

In spite of the general decline of papal authority, the high point of Napoleon Bonaparte's career came in 1804, when Pius VII (Barnaba Chiaramonti) went to Paris to consecrate him emperor. "Napoleon could not regard the popular mandate as a sufficient foundation for the new legitimacy." (Lefebvre 1969, 185.) He still needed the pope's presence to give his act a glimmer of legality in the eyes of the world.

In the 18th and 19th centuries the decline of papal power continued on the world scene. In 1726 Pope Benedict XIII (Pietro Francesco Orsini) gave up his right of investiture to the crown of Sardinia. During Napoleon's reign even the Papal States disappeared for a short time. The Two Sicilies remained nominally a papal fief until 1818, when Pius VII renounced his suzerainty over the kingdom. Another tradition lingered on a little longer: papal nuncios were recognized by the Congress of Vienna as doyens of the diplomatic corps, and thus had precedence over all other ambassadors.

As the call for Italian unification gathered strength, a variety of schemes saw the light of day. On the 20th of July 1858 the Sardinian prime minister Count Camillo Cavour met the Emperor Napoleon III in Plombieres. In a secret understanding they agreed to recognize a unified Italy in the form of a federation of three kingdoms and a papal domain under the overall presidency of the pope. But the plan was eventually derailed.

The popes remained in possession of their earthly kingdom until the final unification of Italy in 1870. On the 20th of September of that year, after the Italian army made a breach at the Porta Pia, Pope Pius IX (Giovanni Mastai-Ferretti), to prevent further bloodshed, ordered the white flag of surrender hoisted on the castle Sant'Angelo. With the incorporation of Rome into the kingdom of Italy, the pontifical armed forces were disbanded, and eleven centuries of papal sovereignty over the Roman States came to an end.

The year 1870 undoubtedly appeared to be the nadir of the modern papacy. The international standing of the Vatican improved considerably under Pope Leo XIII (Gioacchino Pecci) whose socio-political encyclicals provided the ideological foundations for the Christian Democratic parties in Europe and Latin America. The pope's diplomatic stature also increased dramatically when in 1885 he successfully mediated the dispute between Germany and Spain over the possession of the Caroline islands in the Pacific.

The most pressing task for the papacy, however, remained finding a solution to the Roman Question. For the popes it was always an article of faith that the Vicar of Christ must be a sovereign, and can never be the subject of an earthly ruler or a secular state. An independent papal state was considered a prerequisite for the free exercise of papal power. The quest finally bore fruit; the Lateran Treaty of 1929 between Italy and the papacy created the small but independent State of Vatican City, and thus restored the pope to temporal sovereignty.

Today, the pope's the first two crowns, although diminished, survive; but the powers of the third crown, it seems, has been lost forever.

Chapter 3:

The Fountain of Political Legitimacy

The ascension of Pepin the Short to the Frankish throne in 751, with the authorization of Pope Zacharias, followed by the bestowal of the Roman imperial crown on Charlemagne in 800 by Pope Leo III, established the precedents on which the universal political power of the papacy rested. Otto I was the first German king to appeal to the pope for the imperial crown. While he was unsuccessful at the first attempt, he finally received the imperial diadem from Pope John XII in 962.

For many centuries the popes disposed of the crown of the Holy Roman Empire. This part of history was discussed in the previous chapter and is therefore not repeated here.

Since the pope was the fountainhead of imperial power, it was natural for other rulers to petition the papal throne for a royal crown and for recognition of their legitimacy. States like Croatia, Hungary, Poland, Sicily, Portugal, Bulgaria, Serbia, Lithuania, and Jerusalem in Asia Minor, and the Canaries off the coast of Africa, were raised to the rank of kingdoms by papal sanctions.

The reverse was also true, sometimes emperors and kings lost their thrones through papal censure. Thus, Pope Innocent III felt justified in declaring that rulers were "kings by the grace of God and the pope" (Gontard 1964, 267).

In 992 Prince Mieszko, of the house of Piast, Poland's first historic ruler, to counteract German pressure, placed his lands under the protection of Pope John XV. Through most of the Middle Ages Poland remained a vassal state of the Holy See, which assured Polish independence from its neighbors. Pope John XIX, in 1025, raised the country to the status of a kingdom and authorized the coronation of Boleslav I as king of Poland.

After a period of fragmentation, Poland was again elevated to the dignity of a kingdom by Pope Gregory VII, whose legates crowned

Boleslav II in 1076. Three years later, however, when the king had the
bishop of Cracow murdered, the Pope felt compelled to act. He banned
Boleslav and drove him out of the country. After Boleslav II, the Polish
monarchy broke up into a number of independent principalities. The
nation retained its unity only through the ecclesiastical organization,
which remained under papal patronage.

It was only at the end of the 13th century, in 1288, that the ruler of
Cracow, Henry IV, took steps to reconstruct the kingdom of the Piasts.
He immediately petitioned Pope Nicholas IV for the royal crown, but
died before he could realize his plans (Halecki 1976, 45). It was seven
years later that the archbishop of Gniezno crowned, with papal
authorization, Przemyslav II king of Poland. This was, however, a
somewhat premature award because Przemyslav did not rule over the
entire country.

The real restorer of the Polish kingdom was Wladislaus I, (or IV if
we count the rulers of Cracow) who in 1305 succeeded in reuniting
Little and Great Poland. Consequently, Pope John XXII, in 1320,
authorized the reinstitution of the royal dignity.

During the Middle Ages, the popes continued to dispose of the
crowns of the world. In the 13th century, for a short period, Lithuania
also became a kingdom. In 1253, Innocent IV bestowed the royal
crown on Mindaugas of Lithuania, who for a while espoused the papal
cause to escape the political and military pressure of the Teutonic
Knights. He was the first and only king of Lithuania, which later
became a grand duchy and eventually was united with Poland.

The kingdom of Hungary also came into being as a result of papal
sanction. In 1001 Duke Vajk (later St. Stephen) of the house of Árpád,
in an astute political move, petitioned Pope Silvester II for a royal
crown. The pope granted the request, raised the Hungarian leader to
royal rank and sent him the crown that is still the symbol of Hungarian
nationhood. This allowed Hungary to enter the western political system
without admitting the suzerainty of the Holy Roman Empire.

Later, to keep his country independent of German overlordship, King
Géza I of Hungary asked the help of Gregory VII, and in 1074 he
recognized the pope as his feudal suzerain. This shrewd strategy again
halted the attempted extension of imperial sway over the country.

Two hundred years later, however, the papacy had to face a crisis in
Hungary. Ladislas IV "the Cumanian," a wild youth (whose mother was
a Cumanian princess) who favored his pagan friends, so alarmed Pope
Nicholas IV that he decided to replace him, and in 1288 preached a

crusade against him. After being hounded from one end of the country to the other, the king fell to the sword of an assassin. Ladislas was succeeded by Andrew III, the last king of the house of Árpád.

When the dynasty became extinct another crisis arose. The throne was claimed by the Bohemian and Bavarian ruling houses, but Pope Boniface VIII supported Charles Robert (Carobert) of Anjou. As a result of papal patronage, he was crowned in 1301 by the primate of Hungary, but then had to yield to his opponents. A few years later, in 1307, Pope Clement V formally awarded the crown of Hungary to Carobert, who ascended the throne as Charles I (Kelly 1986, 213).

A century later, when Sigismund of Hungary threatened an expedition into Italy in support of his brother Wenceslas, Pope Boniface IX found a way to keep him busy at home. Taking advantage of the discontent with Sigismund's rule, and the popularity of the house of Durazzo, the pope, in 1402, in secret consistory, declared Ladislas of Naples king of Hungary. He was crowned at Zara in the presence of the papal legate, but was later defeated in Hungary and had to withdraw to Naples.

Despite some setbacks, the papal throne continued to be the focus of international adjudication. In Bohemia, George Podiebrad, leader of the Hussites, was elected king in 1459. He was an ambitious and shifty ruler and consequently had a long feud with the papacy. Finally in 1466 Pope Paul II felt compelled to excommunicate the king and order his removal from the throne.

Responding to a papal summons, Matthias of Hungary joined the papal crusade against George, conquered large parts of Moravia, and was elected king by the Catholic magnates. He was crowned at Brunn in 1469.

Another claimant to the throne, however, was Ladislas (Vladislav) of Poland. Both candidates looked to the pope for confirmation of their claims. Paul II, who wished to use both contestants against George, remained noncommittal. In the end Ladislas of Poland (son of Casimir IV), with papal acquiescence, ended up on the throne in 1471. (He also became king of Hungary in 1490.)

During the Middle Ages, the political authority of the papacy was also felt on the Iberian peninsula. In 1068 King Sancho V Ramirez of Aragon placed his country under the protection of Pope Alexander II. One and a half centuries later, Peter II of Aragon also surrendered his kingdom to the Apostolic See and received it back as a papal fief. Pope Innocent III bestowed on him the royal crown in Rome in 1204.

In the middle of the 12th, century the popes also extended their sway over Portugal. In 1143 Pope Innocent II arranged the treaty of Zamora, whereby Castile recognized the independence of Portugal. A year later, after Alfonso promised to pay an annual tribute, Pope Lucius II accepted the country as a fief of the Holy See.

With the help of English, Scandinavian, French and German crusaders bound for Palestine, Alfonso took Lisbon in 1147. In 1179 Pope Alexander III elevated Portugal to the status of an independent kingdom, and confirmed the right of Alfonso I to the crown.

In the following century, however, a crisis arose in Portugal because of the incompetence of King Sancho II. The government deteriorated to such an extent that Pope Innocent IV was compelled to intervene. In 1245 he dethroned the king by papal bull, and offered the crown to his brother, the count of Boulogne, who ascended the throne as Alfonso III. Although Alfonso later had problems with the Holy See because of a bigamous marriage, Pope Urban IV declared his son, Diniz, legitimate.

During the 12th century, papal hegemony was also extended to England. King Stephen owed his throne to papal recognition, when Innocent II ratified his election and upheld his claim against those of the Empress Matilda. Later, however, when the king fell out with Rome over the appointment to the see of York, Pope Eugenius III, in 1151, forbade the English bishops to consecrate his son, Eustace, and the succession was passed to Henry II in 1154.

A year later Henry asked Pope Adrian IV for permission to invade Ireland. The pope was again recognized as the forum that distributes sovereignty over the countries of the world. The English pope accommodated the monarch and in his bull *Laudabiliter* bestowed the overlordship of Ireland on the king of England.

In spite of this papal support, Henry, in 1164, passed the Constitutions of Clarendon in an attempt to check ecclesiastical jurisdiction in England. This started his conflict with Thomas Becket, his former chancellor and now archbishop of Canterbury. After Becket's murder by supporters of the king, Pope Alexander III pulled his iron fist out of the velvet glove and imposed the church's full sanctions on Henry. The king was forced to do public penance and to renounce the Constitutions of Clarendon, to obtain papal absolution.

Pope Innocent III also had his way in England. King John incurred the enmity of the pope when he refused to accept his nominee to the see of Canterbury. Innocent first excommunicated and then, in 1213, formally deposed the king, empowering Philip Augustus of France to execute the sentence.

John had to submit and was forced to cede England and Ireland to the Holy See, and to hand over his crown to the Pope's legate. After the king's complete surrender, Pope Innocent III reinstated him in his realms as a vassal of the Holy See. The king swore fealty to the pope, and committed England to pay a yearly tribute of 1000 marks sterling.

John, however, was an autocratic and unscrupulous ruler. When the barons rebelled against the king in 1214, both sides appealed to the pope for arbitration. King John took the cross to assure himself of papal support, both as a vassal and as a crusader.

Later, when the barons forced the king to issue the *Magna Carta*, Pope Innocent III, as the suzerain of England, annulled the charter on the ground that he, as the feudal overlord of the realm, was not consulted. In this document, the pope saw an insurrection against legitimate royal authority. The *Magna Carta* was later reissued several times with modifications.

The pope, through his legates, ruled England for years during the minority of Henry III. King John had entrusted his son to the protection of the Holy See; as a result, successive papal legates (Gualo and Pandulf) had effective control of the government. Although Edward I refused to pay the feudal fees, it was not until 1366 that Edward III formally ended papal overlordship over the kingdom.

In the 14th century papal policy also affected Scotland. In 1323 Pope John XXII confirmed the royal title of Robert I, the Bruce, even though his predecessor, Clement V, had excommunicated him for the murder of John Comyn, a potential competitor.

In France, since Pepin's assumption of the crown by papal sanction, the popes had to intervene a few times to prop up the wobbling thrones of kings. In 942 Pope Stephen VIII threatened the rebels against Louis IV with ecclesiastical censures, and in 1226 Pope Honorius III had to step in to assure the succession of Louis IX (St. Louis). Later, in 1303, during the feud between Boniface VIII and Philip IV, the pope had planned to proclaim the dethronement of the French king, but Philip beat him to the punch with an attack on the papal palace in Anagni.

Of the feudal kingdoms of the papacy, Naples and Sicily were geographically closest to Rome, and therefore felt the most interference by the papal government. The kingdom was a papal fief since 1059 when Nicholas II invested Robert Guiscard with southern Italy and Sicily. The antipope "Anacletus II" granted the royal title to Roger II of Sicily in 1330, with authority also over Calabria, Apulia, and Naples.

Pope Innocent II confirmed and recognized Roger's title by the treaty of Migniano in 1139.

Later, to counterbalance imperial power, Pope Adrian IV recognized William I as king of Sicily and Naples by the treaty of Benevento in 1156. The king accepted papal suzerainty and promised to pay an annual tribute of 1000 gold pieces. In 1190, Tancred, grandson of Roger II, was elected to the throne to thwart the succession of Henry VI of Germany, who was the husband of Constance, heiress to the kingdom. Tancred was invested by Celestine III, but died in 1192. His death removed the impediment to Henry's acquisition of the kingdom, but the latter still needed papal approval to assume the crown.

When Henry himself died in 1197, his widow Constance became regent in Sicily for her young son, Frederick. She acknowledged papal overlordship over the realm, and at her death made Pope Innocent III guardian of her infant son.

Though Innocent eventually promoted his ward to the imperial throne, the king had first to promise, in 1213 in the Golden Bull of Eger, to respect the territorial integrity of the enlarged Papal States and to keep Sicily independent of the empire. Frederick was at first politically allied with the papacy, but not unduly burdened by conventional piety. In Sicily, he kept an oriental-style harem guarded by eunuchs.

Frederick II, however, was far from giving up his dream of imposing his rule over Italy. It was only a matter of time before his ambitious Italian policy precipitated the final break with the papacy. In 1245 he was deprived of his thrones by Pope Innocent IV, and a few years later Pope Urban IV offered the vacant throne of Sicily to Charles of Anjou, brother of Louis IX of France.

Charles came to take over Naples and Sicily with the privileges of a crusader, and was invested with the kingdom in 1266 by Pope Clement IV. He defeated the last of the Hohenstaufen, but his hold over the island did not last. Widespread popular discontent resulted in a revolt in 1282. The Sicilians called in Peter III of Aragon, who had a claim to the kingdom through his Hohenstaufen wife. Thus, Angevin rule became restricted to Naples.

The papacy naturally could not accept such a challenge to its suzerainty over Sicily, and Pope Nicholas IV in 1289 invested Charles II, son of Charles of Anjou, with the kingdom. Charles, however, ruled only in Naples because the island remained in Aragonese hands. But in 1304 Pope Benedict XI also enforced the allegiance of Frederick III of Sicily (the son of Peter III) and obliged him to pay his tribute for the island kingdom as a vassal of the Holy See.

At the beginning of the Great Schism, Urban VI dethroned Queen Joanna of Naples because she supported the pope in Avignon, and invested Charles of Durazzo with the kingdom. Charles III, in turn, had to invest the pope's nephew, Francesco (Butillo) Prignano, with Capua, Amalfi, Sorrento, and Gaeta, and was then solemnly crowned king of Naples in Rome in 1381. Their amity, however, did not last very long. Four years later the pope laid the kingdom under an interdict.

After Charles' death, Urban even made plans to place Butillo on the throne of Naples, although his nephew clearly lacked the virtues a pope would be expected to admire. Earlier he had forcibly entered a convent and violated a high-born nun well known for her beauty. The pope excused his nephew on account of his age (he was 40) and, as suzerain of the kingdom of Naples, used his position to stop the prosecution. As punishment for the crime, Butillo was condemned to matrimony and received as a dowry the castle of Nocera (Creighton 1897, 1:87).

Unlike his predecessor, the next pope, Boniface IX, was a clear-headed statesman. In 1390 he enfeoffed Ladislas, son of Charles III, with the kingdom of Naples, after receiving his fealty as a vassal of the Holy See. (The pope also invested his own brother, Andrew Tomacelli, with the duchy of Spoleto and the marquisate of Ancona.) The pope supplied Ladislas with funds and mercenaries who, after a long war, defeated the forces Louis of Anjou, backed by the antipope "Clement VII."

During the Middle Ages, papal authority also extended to the Balkans. Ever since Pope John X bestowed the royal crown on Duke Tomislav of Croatia in 925, the country remained in the orbit of Rome. Petar Kresimir (1058-74) was closely allied with the papacy and greatly extended the boundaries of his kingdom. His successor, Demetrius Zvonimir, was crowned king of Croatia at Split in 1076 by a legate of Pope Gregory VII. He joined a papal crusade, but was killed in an insurrection.

Papal hegemony over the country, however, remained paramount. In 1093 Petar Svacic was proclaimed king, but failed to obtain papal recognition. Pope Urban II, who regarded him as a rebel, invited King Koloman of Hungary to remove him from the throne. As a result the Hungarians invaded the country, Petar fell in battle in 1097, and the crown of Croatia was united with that of Hungary.

The popes continued the practice of handing out royal dignities by Apostolic favor. In 1077 Mikhail of Serbia was crowned king by a legate of Pope Gregory VII. Afterwards the country came under Byzantine suzerainty, but then returned for a short time to the papal orbit. Thus, Stephan Nemanya II, in 1217, was also crowned king of Serbia by a legate of Pope Honorius III.

Another ruler who paid homage to the Apostolic See was Kaloyan (Joannitza) of Bulgaria. Pope Innocent III, in the interest of the spiritual and temporal well-being of the country, awarded him the royal title in 1204. Kaloyan swore fealty to the pope as his feudal overlord, promising tribute and military assistance, and was crowned by a papal legate.

The supranational authority of the pope also extended to other continents. Pope Paschal II authorized, in 1100, the establishment of the kingdom of Jerusalem and the assumption of the royal crown by Baldwin I. Pope Clement VI, in 1345, arbitrated claims over the Canary Islands; he awarded the archipelago to Juan de la Cerda of Castile, and performed his royal coronation in Avignon.

In addition (as we shall see in Chapter 5) the popes of the 15th century allocated the continents of the globe to European colonial powers. The kings of Spain and Portugal based the legitimacy of their rule over America, Africa, and parts of Asia on the donation of Pope Alexander VI in the bull *Inter caetera*.

The pope not only surpassed the kings of the world in rank and dignity, his power was different in nature. He did not supplant or rival theirs, but rose above them to become the source of their authority. His power was not territorial (except in the Papal States) but universal and supranational.

The culmination of these papal actions in the Middle Ages converted the papacy into the fountainhead of political legitimacy and "raised the chair of Peter to be the throne of all the world" (Gontard 1964, 270).

Chapter 4:

The Military Policy of the Popes

The Crusading Movement

This chapter does not deal with the detailed history of the crusades. There are many good books available on the subject. This section treats only those aspects of the military campaigns that illustrate the supranational, governmental function of the popes and their coordinated political, ideological and military policies.

In 1049, Pope Leo IX established a Roman militia to protect his territories. A few years later Pope Gregory VII called on laymen to join the Knights of St. Peter, a military organization owing allegiance to the pope, set up to defend the church. These attempts, however, were precursors of the pontifical armed forces, whose duty it was to defend the Papal States, and are therefore outside the scope of the supranational military machinery of the papacy.

From the founding of the caliphate in 632 to the second siege of Vienna in 1683 the West had to defend itself against a Moslem onslaught. The popes considered it part of their mission to take charge of the military efforts to defend the European Christian commonwealth. They grew slowly, and first innocuously, into their military role.

Pope Benedict VIII, of the house of the counts of Tusculum, was an able soldier and administrator. In 1016 he proclaimed a holy war against the Saracens on Sardinia. After a victorious campaign, he bestowed the island on Pisa. Between 1060 to 1090 the Normans, with papal blessing, occupied Sicily. Papal patronage of these conquests were symbolized by the consecrated banners the popes sent the conquerors: in 1017 to the Pisans, and in 1063 to the Normans in Sicily.

These symbolic presentations were continued by the popes. Alexander II sent a banner, in 1064, to the force that captured Barbastro in Spain, and to William the Conqueror, in 1066, for his invasion of England. Victor III also sent a consecrated banner to the Pisan and Genoese fleets that attacked the Saracen stronghold of Mahdia in North Africa in 1087.

Even before the crusades proper, the popes offered indulgences to those who fought for their causes: Alexander II (1061-73) gave absolution to the Normans who fought in Sicily, and offered indulgences to the knights of Aquitaine for fighting in Spain against the Moors.

Slowly the idea of the *ecclesia militans*, the quest to extend the borders of Christendom through force of arms, became an accepted idea, probably to appease the old Germanic bellicosity that found little understanding in the principle of turning the other cheek. But to fight as a vassal of a priestly world emperor for the glory of God found ready acceptance in the feudal atmosphere of the Middle Ages.

The crusading movement also meshed with the emerging papal claim to be the overlord of all earthly rulers, and therefore could channel their military activities in a direction that could help defend the western world. The great crusading armies finally catapulted the papacy into a global power. Only the pope, because of his supranational character, possessed the political, legal, ideological, and military means to organize the defense of the European commonwealth.

The crusading movement is depicted as a wave of intense religious enthusiasm, and it is undeniable that it had deep religious motives as its guiding force. Its origins, however, were more down to earth. When the Turks conquered Asia Minor, the Byzantine emperor, Michael VII, sent an urgent appeal for help to Pope Gregory VII in 1073. The ruler of Constantinople addressed his plea not to the western emperor or any western king, but to the pope, the only supranational power in existence, whose authority was not limited to a piece of real estate, but encompassed the entire western world.

In 1074 Gregory indeed assembled a sizeable army, but the investiture contest intervened and plans had to be altered. Michael VII's successor, Alexius I Comnenus, sent a similar appeal to Pope Urban II. The timing of that request was more propitious and fell on fertile ground. The people learned that Urban would make a pronouncement of immense significance at the Council of Clermont in 1095. So great were the crowds that assembled to hear the pontiff that a platform had to be erected outside of the town.

The people were not disappointed. The pope proclaimed a holy war, the First Crusade, and called on the people of the West to join in the great undertaking for the conquest of Jerusalem, that would also, he hoped, ease the military pressure on the Eastern Empire.

No other speech in history had such a profound and longlasting effect. The response was overwhelming and probably even surprised the pope, who was immediately catapulted into the center stage of world history. As his speech shows, Pope Urban was fired by a holy zeal and vision, but he was also wise in worldly ways and knew how to move the faithful.

Monks, noblemen and peasants knelt before the papal throne and made a pledge to take the cross. (Small crosses were distributed to the people.) Soon a stream of humanity flowed across the Balkans toward the Middle East. Crusading enthusiasm sped like wildfire throughout Europe and determined the course of history for the next two hundred years.

The pope offered plenary indulgences (forgiveness of sins) to all who took the cross, and he placed all crusaders, their families and possessions, under papal protection. This meant that a large segment of the population was freed from the lordship of their feudal masters and became, in effect, subjects of the pope.

Urban II appointed Adhemar, bishop of Le Puy, papal legate and leader of the crusade, but he died early in the campaign, and the crusading armies were led by French knights: Godfrey of Bouillon, his brother Baldwin, Raymond of Toulouse, Bohemond of Otranto, his nephew Tancred, Robert of Normandy, Stephen of Blois, and Robert of Flanders.

To ensure the effective assembling of the crusading armies, Urban II also proclaimed a universal peace in the West. Even before Urban, the popes were always concerned with the lawlessness and constant feudal warfare among the nobles, and therefore adopted the Truce of God, which attempted to enforce the peace on certain days of the week. The pope also looked to the crusading movement as a means of channeling the aggressiveness of kings and knights into a worthy undertaking against an external enemy.

On the surface it is surprising that the church, with its professed aim of maintaining peace in the world, should proclaim a war of conquest. There were situations, however, that required action. Already Gregory VII looked to Anselm of Lucca and St. Augustine of Hippo, who justified violence in certain cases as sanctioned by God. Later, in the 12th century, Gratian, the great compiler of canon law, took the position (Causa XXIII of his *Decretum*) that there was such a thing as a just war and could be authorized on God's behalf by the pope. (Riley-Smith 1987, 93.)

It is difficult, if not impossible, to understand the crusading movement with a 20th century mind. Although if we reflect with how much passion Jerusalem is fought over even today, the undertaking becomes somewhat more comprehensible.

In medieval Europe the dominant organization and all- pervasive social reality was the church; it controlled every aspect of life. Lands constantly changed hands; they were conquered and allocated to different rulers. It is not surprising therefore that people's first loyalty was to the pope, the head of the only universal and stable institution in Europe.

The First Crusade was crowned by success. On the 15th of July 1099 the holy warriors took Jerusalem by storm, followed by a terrible slaughter of the inhabitants. At the end of the day the crusaders assembled in the church of the Holy Sepulchre "clasping their bloodstained hands together in prayer and thanksgiving" (Norwich 1995, 42). The conquest of Jerusalem created a wave of euphoria throughout Europe. The crusaders established the Latin Kingdom of Jerusalem and its fiefs: the counties of Edessa and Tripoli, and the principality of Antioch.

After Adhemar de Puy, the papal legate, had died in 1098, Pope Urban II appointed Daimbert of Pisa as his successor. It was in this capacity that he invested Godfrey of Bouillon with Jerusalem, and Bohemond with Antioch. Godfrey became "Defender of the Holy Sepulchre," the title he chose because he refused to wear a royal crown were Christ had worn a crown of thorns.

After Godfrey's death, Daimbert attempted to establish a patriarchal theocratic state in Jerusalem; but Pope Paschal II, realizing the importance of placing the new state on a military foundation, authorized the assumption of the royal crown by Baldwin I, who was not burdened by his brother's scruples. He was crowned king of Jerusalem in 1100 by the patriarch.

The constant infighting and the fragmentation of authority, however, greatly weakened the crusader states. Setbacks necessarily followed, culminating in the fall of Edessa in 1144. On hearing the news, Pope Eugenius III immediately issued the encyclical *Quantum praedecessores,* initiating the Second Crusade. The king of France, Louis VII, and the king of Germany, Conrad III, took crusading vows. Other crusaders from Holland, Scandinavia and England, on the way to Palestine, captured Lisbon from the Moors and thus helped establish Portugal.

Once in the Middle East, the kings attacked, but failed to take, Damascus. The reverses continued. The rise of Saladin, a leader of genius, coincided with anarchy in the crusader states. Guy de Lusignan, who succeeded King Baldwin V, was no match for the Saracen leader who, in 1187, launched his long awaited *Jihad* for the recapture of Jerusalem.

Saladin's victory at Hattin over the crusaders presaged the fall of Jerusalem. At the battle of the Horns of Hattin, Saladin's men vowed to teach the Christians a lesson. If this is true, their remarks were ironic, because the world had already learned a lesson in those hills. According to some accounts, it was the site of the Sermon on the Mount. (Howarth 1982, 153.)

Jerusalem capitulated on the 2nd of October 1187. After an absence of 88 years, the green banner of the Prophet again fluttered over the holy city. The news of its loss shocked the western world, forcing Pope Gregory VIII to issue the encyclical *Audita tremendi,* proclaiming the Third Crusade. He sent his legates all over Europe to preach it. Frederick Barbarossa of Germany, Philip Augustus of France, and Richard I of England took the cross in 1188.

The crusade got under way in 1189 in the reign of Pope Clement III. It was probably the largest crusading army, estimated at 100,000 men. On the way to Palestine, Richard I conquered Cyprus and thus founded another crusader state that he first sold to the Templars and then to Guy de Lusignan.

After a two-year siege the crusaders finally reconquered Acre, but national differences, dissension among the crusaders, and conflicts about the succession to the kingdom caused another failure. Jerusalem was not retaken. Only Antioch and Tripoli and a strip of land along the coast remained in the hands of the crusaders.

News of the failure to take Jerusalem spurred Europe to renewed activity. All levels of society continued to be obsessed by crusading. In 1195, Pope Celestine III called for another campaign, to which Henry VI of Germany responded by dispatching a large army that occupied Sidon and Beirut. This effort ended in 1197, when news of the king's death arrived.

By this time the crusading movement had a life of its own. Pope Innocent III, the most powerful pontiff in history, launched the Fourth Crusade in 1202. All the major powers of the west were bogged down by internal problems, but that did not worry the pope. Innocent was well aware "that Kings and princes, stirring up as they invariably did national rivalries and endless questions of precedence and protocol" (Norwich 1995, 165) were one of the main causes of the failures of the past. The chief participants of the new campaign were French noblemen, the lords of Champagne, Flanders, and Blois.

The attack was to be directed at Egypt, the center of Moslem power. The Venetians, who were to provide the galleys, demanded 85,000 marks and half of the conquests to be made. Since the money was not available, the crusaders made a deal with the Doge Enrico Dandolo and attacked and delivered to Venice the Adriatic city of Zara, which belonged to the king of Hungary, also a crusader and therefore theoretically under papal protection.

After Zara was taken, another complication arose. Alexius, the son of the deposed and blinded Byzantine emperor, Isaac Angelus, escaped from prison, and made an offer to the crusaders. If they would help him overthrow his usurping uncle, Alexius III Angelus, he would finance the crusade and support it with 10,000 soldiers. He would also submit the eastern church to the authority of the pope.

The crusaders were well aware of the immense wealth of Constantinople. "And to any medieval army, whether or not it bore the cross of Christ on its standard, a fabulously rich city meant only one thing: loot" (Norwich 1995, 171). It was an offer the crusaders could not refuse. At first, after the city was taken, the crusaders did install their protégés. But when a *coup d'etat* eliminated Alexius and his father Isaac, the crusaders got tired of Byzantine intrigues and sacked the city.

The laws of war were allowed free reign in the capital of the Eastern Empire, but the rights of pillage were somewhat mitigated by a twist of civility introduced by the victors. The marquis of Montferrat and the count of Flanders, both paragons of virtue, prohibited the rape of matrons, virgins, and nuns by the holy warriors (Gibbon 1960, 779).

The crusaders installed Baldwin IX of Flanders as the first emperor of the newly created Latin Empire of Constantinople, which lasted from 1204 to 1261, and contained several vassal states: the kingdom of Thessalonica (under Boniface of Montferrat), the duchy of Athens (under Otto de la Roche), and the principality of Achaia (under Geoffroy de Villehardouin). Some of these states remained under their

Frankish rulers well into the 15th century.

Thus, new crusader states came into being. Pope Innocent III first disapproved these diversions, but eventually yielded to the appeals of the crusaders, and ratified the conquests. After the death of Baldwin's brother and successor, Henry, Peter de Courteney inherited the imperial throne and was crowned emperor of the Latin Empire in Rome in 1217 by Pope Honorius III.

The coronation, however, was performed outside the walls of the city, because the pope feared that a traditional coronation in St. Peter's could result in the new emperor's claim to the Western Empire as well. It was all in vain. Peter never made it to the throne of Constantinople; he was captured by the despot of Epirus and died in a dungeon.

Since the Fourth Crusade never reached the Holy Land, Pope Innocent III at the Lateran Council of 1215, where representatives of all European rulers were assembled, proclaimed the Fifth Crusade (1218-21). To ensure its success, he decreed a truce for four years all over Europe, and interdicted trade in war materials with the Moslems.

Further, the pope exempted crusaders from tolls, taxes and feudal services, and declared a moratorium on their debts. In 1199, Popes Innocent III imposed a three-year tax on the clergy, amounting to a twentieth of all church income. This precedent assured future popes more control over the crusading movement by becoming its bankers.

One must to remember that concurrently with the campaigns in the Middle East, there were other crusades in different parts of the world. The popes had firmly established their right to authorize the wars — since they alone could grant indulgences — and instituted the practice of issuing crusade encyclicals.

During the Second Crusade, for example, Pope Eugenius III also approved the request of King Alfonso VII of Castile to extend the crusade to Spain, and called on the Genoese and the French to join the enterprise. In 1147 he also authorized military operations against the Wends east of the Elbe. Crusades authorized by the popes were also in progress in the Baltic.

By financing the crusades through taxes, and by manipulating the indulgences and other inducements, the popes were in a position to channel the crusading energy into areas that in their view had priority. When Innocent III was planning the Fifth Crusade, for example, he demoted, in 1214, the crusades in Spain and Languedoc. He was concerned about the fragmentation of effort by having several military campaigns simultaneously. In response to Spanish complains that this will slow the reconquest, he reissued the indulgences, but restricted them to Spaniards.

As the Fifth Crusade got under way, Emperor Frederick II (who later excused himself several times), King Andrew of Hungary, the king of Cyprus, and the dukes of Austria and Bavaria took the cross with a host of crusaders from western Europe. The pope again designated Egypt, the main seat of Moslem power, as the target of the attack. To keep proceedings firmly in his hands, and to eliminate diversionary tactics and the rivalry of kings, Innocent III appointed the papal legate Pelagius as the military leader of the campaign.

Military and naval operations started in 1218 and resulted in the capture of Damietta. John of Brienne, king of Jerusalem, who quarreled with Pelagius and left the scene, was ordered in 1221 by the pope to rejoin the crusade. After waiting in vain for Frederick II, Pelagius, against the advice of John of Brienne, gave the order to march on Cairo. The campaign turned out to be a disaster. Pelagius, after refusing quite generous offers from Malik al-Kamil, finally had to evacuate Damietta in return for a safe retreat.

What came to be known as the Sixth Crusade (1228-29) was not a crusade at all. The Emperor Frederick II, at his coronation as German king in 1215, promised the pope to go on a crusade. Later, in 1225, at St. Germano, he also agreed to maintain 1000 knights in Palestine, at his own expense for two years. He further agreed to provide 100 transports and 50 armed galleys for the crusaders. But Frederick postponed his crusade so often that Gregory IX lost patience and placed him under the papal ban.

When Frederick finally did go to Palestine, the world came to witness the spectacle of an excommunicated emperor acquiring, not by fighting, but by negotiating, Jerusalem, Bethlehem, Nazareth, and a strip of land connecting them to the crusader-held coastal towns. Naturally, none of the military-religious orders of chivalry supported the emperor's "crusade."

Frederick returned to Europe, when he learned that papal armies had invaded his kingdom of Sicily. In any case, the truce he concluded with the sultan of Egypt was due to expire in 1239. In anticipation Pope Gregory IX issued another call for a crusade in 1234.

A large contingent of French knights under the count of Champagne and the duke of Burgundy sailed for Palestine. From England, Richard, earl of Cornwall, brother of king Henry III, sailed with a host of

English knights. After a period of truce, the crusaders allied themselves with the Moslem ruler of Damascus against the sultan of Egypt. As a result, they were defeated by Bibars at Gaza in 1244, and Jerusalem was lost for the last time.

News of the fall of Jerusalem produced the Seventh Crusade, proclaimed by Pope Innocent IV at the Council of Lyons in 1245. Paradoxically, at the same council, Innocent IV deposed Emperor Frederick II and promoted a crusade against him, promising those who took up arms against Frederick the same rewards as were given teh crusaders going to the East. Before, we witnessed nobles using the crusades for political ends, now we see the papacy pursuing the same strategy.

Innocent IV induced Louis IX (St. Louis) of France to lead the expedition to the Middle East. A force of about 15,000 men from France, Germany, England and Scandinavia sailed east, attacked Egypt and took Damietta in 1249. But the disaster of the Fifth Crusade repeated itself. Louis IX was taken prisoner and was ransomed by the Templars. The king then went to Acre, but he accomplished nothing and returned to France in 1254.

After the recapture of Constantinople by the Byzantines in 1261, Pope Urban IV planned a crusade to reconquer it, but soon determined to switch the effort to Syria and Palestine. James I of Aragon, at the urging of the pope, interrupted his Spanish crusade in 1269 for a foray to the east, but only his followers reached Acre.

Despite his previous experience, Louis IX of France was still fired up by the crusading zeal. As the leader of the Eighth Crusade, he left Aigues-Mortes in 1270 and joined the crusading fleet in Sardinia for the attack on Tunis in North Africa. Soon after landing, however, he became ill and died. His brother, Charles of Anjou, ended the affair with a treaty with the bey of Tunis.

Prince Edward of England (later King Edward I), who arrived in Tunis after the French king died, continued to Acre but, due to a truce between Egypt and the kingdom of Jerusalem, accomplished little. This ended the last of the classic crusades in history.

Notwithstanding the lack of results, the popes kept trying. The Visconti pope, Gregory X, convened the second Council of Lyons in 1274 and called for a crusade. The kings of France and Sicily took the cross in 1275 and the kings of England and Aragon agreed to join. The German king, Rudolph of Habsburg, also planned to join in return for the pope's promise to bestow on him the imperial crown.

The hard-pressed Byzantine emperor, Michael VIII Paleologus, promised his support and even agreed to unify the Orthodox church with Rome, in order to save his throne. But the pope died in 1276 and the vast enterprise died with him.

By that time, the kingdom of Jerusalem was tottering. Quarrels among the crusaders hastened its fall. Infighting and rivalries took their toll. In 1291 Acre, the last stronghold of the crusaders in Palestine, fell to Sultan Khalil, and with it the kingdom of Jerusalem passed into history.

The crusades represent a flaring up of idealism that for centuries continued to tug at the soul of Europe. There is no doubt that many joined from noble motives, but the crusading armies also harbored many less desirable elements. St. Bernard of Clairvaux, the most eloquent preacher of the Second Crusade, was not overly impressed by what he saw. He commented that the crusades may do some good for two reasons: they may recapture the Holy Land, and they will definitely rid Europe of a lot of "scoundrels, vagabonds, thieves, murderers, perjurers and adulterers" (Binns 1995, 103).

It was through the crusades that the popes removed the Holy Roman emperors, to whom they once had granted the headship of the world, and claimed that position for themselves. In fact, sometimes they directed a crusade against the empire itself. With the destruction of the house of Hohenstaufen, the papacy achieved its victory over its own creation, the Holy Roman Empire.

In 20th century parlance, we may characterize the crusades as a policy of containment. As the Moslem world was encroaching on the bastions of Europe from the east, the south and southwest, the papacy was the only world power at the time capable of mounting a massive military undertaking that united all of Europe for a common cause.

Even after the classic age of the crusades came to an end, military campaigns continued in Spain and North Africa, and ended with the Holy Leagues against the Ottoman Empire, sponsored by the popes and supported by crusader bulls in the 16th and 17th centuries, until the final roll- back of Turkish power in the 18th century.

The crusades tremendously increased the power of the papacy. The crusading movement, which dominated the history of Europe for centuries, was launched by the popes, was financed to a large extent by the popes, and was sometimes led by papal legates. It was the first great military undertaking in which the papal throne united the feudal society of the West for a common cause.

Expanding the Frontiers of the European Commonwealth

The military policy of the papacy opened new frontiers for Europe. While the crusades went on in the Middle East, there were other theaters of war, where the armies were supported by papal letters and privileges. There is some evidence that already Urban II, when he promoted the First Crusade, authorized indulgences for Spaniards who fought for the reconquest of Terragona (Riley-Smith 1987, 6).

A campaign to liberate the Balearic Islands, supported by crusading letters and privileges granted by Pope Pascal II, was begun in 1114. A year later, Pope Eugenius III authorized King Alfonso VII of Castile to launch a crusade in Spain. Another crusade was proclaimed in 1118 by Pope Gelasius II and led by Alfonso I of Aragon for the reconquest of Saragossa. Pope Calixtus II promoted military campaigns in Spain in 1123, granting the crusaders the same indulgences as to the ones going to Syria and Palestine.

Other military operations in Spain were authorized by the popes in 1153, 1157, and 1175. This period also witnessed the creation of the Spanish military-religious orders (Calatrave, Santiago, Alcantara) which played a prominent role in the wars of the reconquest of Spain.

In 1189 fleets of Danish, Flemish, English, and German crusaders on the way to Palestine helped the king of Portugal to take Silves and Alver. The popes continued to press for the reconquest of the Iberian peninsula. Pope Celestine III issued crusade encyclicals for Spain in 1193 and 1197. The latter was prompted by the victory of the Almohad Caliph Ya'qub at Alarcos in 1195 (Riley-Smith 1987, 139).

In response to the successes of the Caliph Muhammad al- Nassir, Pope Innocent III proclaimed a new crusade in Spain in 1212. Alfonso VIII of Castille, Peter II of Aragon, and Sancho VII of Navarre all participated. The Almohad army was decisively defeated at Las Navas de Tolosa, which was a turning point in the reconquest. In 1218 Honorius III also launched a crusade against the Moors in Spain. Another crusading letter with full indulgences for the Iberian theater of operations was issued by Pope Gregory IX in 1229.

The popes had long realized that the Almohad Empire expanding in southwestern Europe posed just as great a threat as the Turkish menace in the east. In the 1230s crusading privileges were granted to those who helped the Spanish military-religious orders in the reconquest. King

James of Aragon led crusades to Majorca and Valencia. Pope Innocent IV authorized a crusade in 1246 for the reconquest of Seville, which fell to Ferdinand III of Castile two years later.

Expectations ran high. A crusade was even preached to invade Africa, but it petered out; Alfonso X of Castille succeeded in 1260 only to hold Sale on the Atlantic coast of Morocco for a few days. Alfonso XI, king of Castile from 1312 to 1350, was one of the most successful crusaders in Spain in the 14th century; he died during the siege of Gibraltar. With the proliferation of papal grants and the allocation of crusader tenths to finance the war effort, the pressure mounted on the Moslem holdings on the Iberian peninsula.

With the marriage of Ferdinand of Aragon and Isabella of Castile, crusading enthusiasm against the Moors in Spain received another boost. A series of campaigns, supported by the popes with encyclicals and crusader privileges, finally led to the conquest of Grenada in 1492. With papal authorization the war was continued on the coast of North Africa, reviving the old idea of reaching Palestine that way. Oran fell in 1509 and Tripoli a year later.

The popes were also concerned with maintaining security of the shipping lanes. The Farnese Pope, Paul III, preached a crusade in 1534 against the Barbary pirates who constantly threatened shipping in the Mediterranean. The Emperor Charles V himself led assaults on Tunis and Algier. Popes Paul IV and Pius IV also promoted military operations in North Africa; in 1560 about 90 vessels with German, French, Spanish and Italian crusaders sailed for, conquered and held for a while the Island of Jerba.

The crusades in the 16th century spilled over into the western parts of Africa. King Sebastian of Portugal was completely imbued with the idea of a holy war. He invaded Morocco in company of the papal legate and suffered a crashing defeat at Al Kasr al Kebir in 1578, where he died. His forces consisted of about 16,000 men from all parts of Europe, including a small papal army under Sir Thomas Stukeley originally destined for Ireland (Riley-Smith, 246).

The Iberian powers were naturally more interested in North Africa than in the eastern Mediterranean, and papal policy, realizing the strategic importance of the southern and western flanks of Europe, made allowances for this.

Concurrently with the wars in Spain and Portugal, another theater of operations opened up in northern Europe. Pope Alexander III around 1171 authorized a crusade against the Slavs, Estonians, and Fins. King

Valdemar II of Denmark led a campaign against the Estonians, and the Danish fleet attacked Sarena in 1206 as part of a papal crusade.

A grateful Pope Innocent III actually saved the earlier German conquests of Valdemar from reconquest by Emperor Otto IV, by threatening to excommunicate any German prince who attacked the Danish ruler. Pope Honorius III, uneasy about incursions from Novgorod, promised Valdemar possession of all the lands he conquered. The Danes then mounted another military operation in Estonia and established a settlement at Tallin.

In 1107, King Sigurd of Norway went on a crusade, but his destination was the Middle East. He stopped in England, France, and Spain, where he fought against the Moors. The king reached Acre in 1110 and helped Baldwin I of Jerusalem conquer Sidon.

Eric IX of Sweden, as a result of a call for a crusade by Pope Adrian IV, conquered Finland around 1155. Christianity, however, was not firmly established there until half a century later. Thomas, an English bishop, in 1209 almost separated Finland from Sweden to establish it as a papal province.

In 1193 and 1197 Pope Celestine III also granted indulgences to those fighting in the Baltic. Albert of Buxtehude established the Brothers of the Sword in 1202 and actually carved out an ecclesiastical state around Riga under the direct authority of the pope. In a bull of 1204 Innocent III proclaimed the same indulgences for those fighting in the Baltic as for crusaders going to Syria and Palestine. This set the stage for the later conquest of Livonia and Estonia.

The most formidable holy warriors in the Baltic region, however, were the Teutonic Knights. In 1225 Duke Conrad of Mazovia called in the German military-religious crusading society that operated in the Middle East under papal charter. The knights had large holdings in Palestine, centered around their castle of Montfort. With their transfer to the Baltic started the German penetration of north-eastern Europe. The knights soon conquered large areas of Prussia and established a powerful domain.

To safeguard their sovereignty from all earthly powers, the German warrior monks in 1234 transferred all their holdings to the Holy See, and received them back from Pope Gregory IX as a papal fief. In 1245 Pope Innocent IV granted plenary indulgences to all Germans who responded to the appeals of the Teutonic Knights to fight in Prussia.

Königsberg fell to the knights in 1254 as a result of a crusading expedition by King Ottokar II of Bohemia, Rudolf of Habsburg, and

Otto of Brandenburg. In 1308 they conquered Pomerania and Danzig. In 1309 Grand Master Siegfried von Feuchtwangen took up residence in Marienburg in East Prussia. The pope gave the order the right to wage a perpetual crusade for the consolidation of the Baltic lands. Many people from other parts of Europe joined the Teutonic Knights for their summer crusades; among them were John of Bohemia, the future Henry IV of England, and Albert of Austria.

The expansion of the Teutonic Knights came to a halt in 1410, when a Polish-Lithuanian army defeated them at Tannenberg. From then on they were on a steady decline. The knights defended Livonia in 1501 against a Russian invasion, and asked Pope Alexander VI for a crusade encyclical, but, significantly, it was denied. The pope was hoping to enlist Russia in the war against the Turks. Crusading in the Baltic was clearly coming to an end (Riley-Smith 1987, 215).

The defense of Europe against attacks by outsiders was always in the forefront of the military policy of the popes. In 1241, when Poland and Hungary were overrun by the Mongols under Batu Khan, the grandson of Genghis Khan, Pope Gregory IX proclaimed a crusade against the Asian conquerors. The king of Poland, Henry II, one of the leaders of the campaign, died in the battle of Lignica. Pope Innocent IV also pursued a diplomatic initiative and in 1246 sent a papal envoy, John of Plano Carpini, to the Mongol court.

When another threat was perceived in 1249, Pope Innocent IV permitted crusaders to the Middle East to convert their vows to fighting the Mongol hordes from Asia. Pope Alexander IV also proclaimed a crusade against them. In the 14th century the popes issued several crusade letters to the Poles and to the Hungarians aimed at halting the Mongol tide.

External enemies, however, were not the only antagonists the papacy had to face. As early as 1135 Pope Innocent II, at the Council of Pisa, decreed that those who fought the pope's enemies shall enjoy the same indulgences granted by Urban II to the crusaders. Thus the stage was set for the later political crusades in Europe against those who challenged the universal hegemony of the papal throne. One of the pope's chief antagonists in the contest for the dominion of the world was the Emperor Frederick II.

The first military campaign against Frederick was launched by Pope Gregory IX in 1239. After a period of uneasy peace, Gregory's successor, Pope Innocent IV, at the Council of Lyons, formally deposed Frederick II from the throne of the empire, and renewed the crusade against him. Many crusaders helped William of Holland, whom the pope had set up as antiking in Germany, capture the imperial capital of Aachen in 1248.

A century later Popes John XXII and Clement VI also had a drawn out conflict with Louis IV, elected German king in 1314, until Clement declared him forfeit of the imperial throne in 1346.

In order to pay the heavy expenses for these war efforts, the popes had to augment the regular crusade taxes with taxes on the first year's income on the new holders of benefices and on income from benefices during vacancies. The popes were very much aware of the growing criticism of using crusades for political ends, but in their view it was just as important to defend the Papal Commonwealth from internal foes as it was from enemies without.

There was no shortage of challengers to papal hegemony. The Albigensian heresy in the south of France started as a religious dispute, but soon turned into a political contest. Innocent III was trying for many years, by peaceful means, to control the dissension. Only when in 1208 the papal legate in Languedoc was assassinated with the complicity, as Innocent suspected, of Count Raymond IV of Toulouse, did the pope decide on military intervention.

In the cultural atmosphere of the Middle Ages, heretics were considered disturbers of the established social order. In the pope's view, when the universal Christian commonwealth was threatened, internally or externally, armed force must be used to protect it.

As the papal crusade gathered strength, the count of Toulouse was speedily reconciled with the pope and endured penitential whipping. The pontiff first appointed Simon de Montfort as the military leader of the operation, but in 1226, in response to a call from Pope Honorius III, King Louis VIII of France took command of the war. The campaign ended with the peace of Paris in 1229. Afterwards the Inquisition assured ideological orthodoxy.

Two centuries later, at the end of the Great Schism, much of the pope's military efforts were still diverted to ensuring religious orthodoxy in Europe. One constant irritation for the popes was Bohemia. Martin V felt compelled to proclaim a crusade against the Hussites and Wycliffites, which was read by his legate at the imperial diet at Wroclaw (Breslau) in 1420.

The Bohemian crusades were perhaps the most futile wars conducted against heretics. The Hussites valiantly held their ground. After several campaigns, the struggle ended in a compromise, which recognized

Sigismund as king of Bohemia.

For many centuries, crusades launched by the popes dominated the center stage of history. The military policy of the popes attempted to protect the flanks of Europe from external enemies and to ensure ideological unity inside the continent. Slowly, however, the world changed and men changed. The Reformation disrupted the unity and the social order of the western world, and by the 17th century only the popes and the rulers hard pressed by the Turks showed any enthusiasm for crusading.

Wars of Containment Against the Ottoman Empire

Even though the classic age of the crusades to the Middle East ended with the fall of Acre in 1291, there were other enterprises that had the character of crusades in the 14th century and beyond, organized by the popes to repel the Ottoman invasion of Europe. In this period, papal policy was mainly concerned with the defense of the eastern settlements and with the enforcement of the naval blockade against Egypt, which was the center of Moslem power. The success of the latter was considered a prerequisite to any possible renewal of a large-scale invasion of the east.

Pope Boniface VIII tightened the rules of the trade embargo, and Clement V empowered the Hospitalers of Rhodes to enforce the blockade of Egypt and to capture suspect ships and sequester their cargoes. From 1320, merchants who traded with the Memelukes were excommunicated, and trading companies were instructed to promulgate rules in accordance with the papal decree.

With the appearance of the Mongols in Europe, the Italian merchants, who saw their trade relations with Asia disrupted by this newest invasion, finally obtained trading licenses from Pope Clement VI, who had by that time given up hope for the recovery of Palestine. From 1344 several licenses were issued by the popes.

Earlier in the century, in 1306, the French Pope Clement V authorized the collection of crusade tenths in France and Naples for a campaign of Charles of Valois for the recovery of the Latin Empire of Constantinople. The trial of the Templars in this period, however, was not very conducive for the planning of a crusade. In spite of that situation, a large group of about 40,000 men from England, France, and Germany gathered in Avignon in 1309 and sailed to the East mainly to help the Hospitalers of Rhodes.

In 1310 Clement V again granted crusader tenths and indulgences for the campaign of Philip of Taranto to protect Latin Greece. Throughout Europe many members of the high nobility had taken the cross, but for one reason or another the efforts remained still-born. There were, nevertheless, limited successes. One naval force, consisting of papal, Venetian, Cypriot and Hospitaler vessels, defeated the Turkish fleet in 1344 and took the port city of Smyrna.

Pope Urban V, prompted by Peter de Lusignan, king of Cyprus, proclaimed another crusade against the Turks in 1363, and named King John II of France as captain-general of the crusading forces. Although The king of France died, King Louis I of Hungary defeated the Turks in 1366, and Peter de Lusignan captured Alexandria and held it for a short time. Later, Count Amadeus of Savoy also succeeded in conquering Gallipoli.

In spite of these partial successes, the pressure on the Eastern Empire kept mounting. In 1369, the Byzantine Emperor John V arrived in Rome to ask the pope for military assistance against the Turks. History has repeated itself. But this time crusading took a different turn. From this time on, the purpose of the campaigns was not so much conquests in the Middle East, but the defense of Europe from the Ottoman Turks.

During the following centuries, several popes, by issuing crusader bulls and organizing alliances, tried to halt the advance of the expanding Ottoman Empire. Again the pope, as the only supranational authority on the continent, attempted to unite Europe for the common defense.

Under Pope Gregory XI (1370-78) the growing threat of the Turks to the European commonwealth began to dominate papal policy. In 1390 "Clement VII," the first antipope of the Great Schism, authorized a crusade that attacked Mahdia in Tunisia under the leadership of Louis II of Clermont, but the invasion ended in failure.

The Roman Pope, Boniface IX, also tried to galvanize the West and proclaimed another crusade in 1394 to repulse the Turks. King Sigismund of Hungary (and future emperor) assumed the supreme command. A large force consisting of Hungarians, Germans, French, Englishmen, and Burgundians, supported by naval squadrons from Venice, Genoa, and the Knights of Rhodes, met the armies of Sultan Bayazid at Nicopolis in 1396 and suffered a crashing defeat. The future

did not bode well.   It was the first test between the West and the
Ottoman sultans.

Although a few years later John Boucicaut succeeded in breaking
the Turkish blockade of Constantinople, the pressure on the Balkans
was relentless. At the Council of Florence in 1439 the Byzantine
emperor, John VII, agreed to unite the Orthodox Church with Rome to
gain papal support against the invading Turks. Once again the ruler of
the Eastern Empire attempted to buy his security by offering his
submission to the papal throne.

Still smarting from a series of defeats at the hands of the Turks,
Pope Eugenius IV in 1443 proclaimed another war against the Ottoman
Empire. A crusading force under Cardinal Cesarini, Wladislaus
(Ulaszlo) of Hungary, and John Hunyadi achieved some successes and
forced the sultan to sue for peace. The peace, however, was not
approved by the pope, and he absolved the king of Hungary from
honoring it.

As a result, the crusade was resumed and a large force of about
20,000 men under Wladislaus of Hungary besieged the town of Varna
on the Black Sea, while a fleet of papal, Venetian, and Byzantine
vessels sailed up the Dardanelles. Again the numerically superior
Turkish army under Sultan Murad defeated the western forces. Both,
the king of Hungary and the papal legate died at the battle of Varna in
1444. It was a devastating blow from which the morale of the western
world never recovered.

The reverses sealed the fate of Constantinople. Sultan Mohammed
II was determined to pluck the greatest prize of his conquests and
spared no effort to boost the morale of his troops. Bands of dervishes
visited the tents, exhorting the soldiers for martyrdom, and assuring
them of the eternal joys of paradise "in the embraces of the black-eyed
virgins" (Gibbon 1960, 841). The sultan also promised them the earthly
rewards of loot and flesh-and-blood maidens.

The last Byzantine emperor, Constantin XI Paleologus, fell, sword
in hand, as the 250,000 men strong Turkish army swarmed into the city
through a breach at the Kerkoporta.   On the 28th of May 1453
Constantinople fell, and Mohammed the Conqueror entered in triumph
the capital of the Eastern Empire.

The fall of Constantinople, the last bulwark that stood between the
continent and the Asian conquerors, jolted the pope and sent
shockwaves all over Europe. True to his word to help the Greeks,
Nicholas V sent a large papal fleet to relieve the siege, but it arrived

Sultan Selim I died in 1520, but his successor, Suleiman I (the Magnificent) continued his strategy of conquest. In 1526 the army of Louis II of Hungary was annihilated in the battle of Mohacs, which sealed the fate of the country for the next 150 years. The second Medici pope, Clement VII, made some efforts to stem the tide, but his precarious relationship with the Emperor Charles V made effective countermeasures difficult.

The rapid spread of Protestantism paralyzed western efforts to repulse the Turks. The pope himself considered the march of Protestantism as a disruption of the social fabric and therefore just as serious a threat as the Ottoman advance in the Balkans. With the 16th and 17th centuries we also see a weakening of the supranational power of the papacy at the expense of *Realpolitik*. In this period the kings of France more or less encouraged the Ottoman sultan in his assault on the empire in order to maintain the geopolitical balance in central Europe.

It was not until later in the 16th century, in 1571, that Pope Pius V succeeded in bringing about a Holy League that carried some punch. The combined Spanish, Venetian and papal fleet, consisting of over 240 vessels, completely destroyed the Turkish navy in the battle of Lepanto, the greatest naval battle since Actium. The popes tried to keep the momentum going. Twenty-five years later Clement VIII sent a 10,000 men strong papal force under the command of his nephew, John Aldobrandini, to Hungary, which achieved some successes.

In the following century, in 1684, after the second siege of Vienna, the Odescalchi pope, Innocent XI, formed another Holy League, consisting of the emperor, Poland, and Venice, supported by a crusader bull, which finally broke the Ottoman power in Europe. Buda, Belgrade and Athens fell to the forces of the league. While there were later reverses, Hungary, where Innocent XI is known as the "liberator pope," was permanently freed from Turkish domination.

Pope Innocent XI made numerous efforts to include France in the alliance. Simultaneously with the land campaign, he wanted the French fleet to attack Constantinople from the sea. Innocent even offered the imperial crown of the Eastern Roman Empire to Louis XIV of France, if he would join the Holy League and thus cause the Ottoman Empire to collapse (Fraknoi 1886, 37).

According to some historians, if France had joined the league, "there can be little doubt that Turkey would have been expelled from Europe" (Ogg 1960, 470). While this did not happen, the Holy League brought about by Innocent XI was definitely the most successful of all the papal

two days after the city was taken and plundered. Th
discourage the pope; he proclaimed another crusade 1
of the capital of the East.

Nicholas' successor, the first Borgia Pope, Calixtus 1
to all the countries of Europe, granted indulgences, impo.
taxes, and set the date for March 1456 for the depai
crusading army. There were some initial successes. A crusac
27,000 men under John Capistrano and John Hunyadi suc
breaking the Turkish blockade of Belgrade, and in 1457 a lar
fleet occupied some of the islands in the Aegean Sea.

In the West, pious support for the defensive campaigns conti
but real resolve was slacking. Of the princes of Europe, only the
of Hungary, whose country felt the main thrust of the Otto
expansion, showed any firm determination for a crusade.

The next pope, Pius II Piccolomini, at the Congress of Mantua
obtained the agreement of the rulers of Europe to observe a general
peace so that they could contribute to the proposed crusade. He wanted
to lead the expedition himself in 1464 to reconquer Constantinople, but
he died at Ancona and the crusade died with him.

After the fall of Negroponte in Greece in 1470, Pope Paul II again
called for crusade, and made an alliance against the Ottoman sultan with
the Iranian prince Uzun-Hassan. In spite of all these efforts the Turkish
advance continued. When Otranto in the south of Italy was seized by
the Turks, Sixtus IV launched another campaign against the Ottoman
Empire, but after retaking Otranto, the papal fleet returned home.

As the liberation of Spain has shown, the papal war strategies in the
west turned out to have more permanent results than in the east, where
most of the effort was concentrated. But the danger from the east was
real and the popes pressed on. Innocent VIII and Alexander VI made
both diplomatic and military initiatives, but the results were minimal.

The Medici pope, Leo X, proclaimed another crusade in 1517 for
which he imposed a three-year tax on benefices. He also decreed a
five-year truce in Europe, and sent legates to all the countries to enforce
it. The Holy Roman Empire, France, England, Venice, and Spain all
heeded the pope's call. In spite of all this diplomatic activity, the effort
petered out and the crusade never materialized.

The Reformation deflected much of the energy of Europe and the
constant contest of the powers for Italian possessions interfered. Only
in eastern Europe, which felt the brunt of the onslaught of the Ottoman
Turks, were crusades still popular.

efforts to free the West from the Ottoman threat. Thus ended the Turkish dream of conquest.

The Papal Military Orders of Chivalry

The three great military-religious orders of chivalry that operated during the Middle Ages under papal charter must be considered the first supranational armies in history. They owed no fealty to any prince, king, or emperor; their only allegiance was to the pope. They were the western world's best disciplined and most formidable fighting forces and fought the pope's wars in Europe, Asia and Africa.

In our time it may seem absurd to speak of warrior monks, but our own cultural environment cannot be a model and made to fit premodern times. The great prestige of the military- religious orders was probably due to the fact that they combined the two great all-consuming passions of the Middle Ages: war and worship.

The Knights Templar (Poor Knights of Christ of the Temple of Solomon) were formed in 1119 for the purpose of protecting the pilgrims to Jerusalem and guarding the public roads in Palestine. Thus, their mission was basically that of peacekeeping. Unlike the Knights Hospitalers and the Teutonic Knights, the Templars were a military order from the very beginning. They followed the Benedictine rule, vowing poverty, chastity and obedience and were committed "to fight with a pure mind for the supreme and true king."

At the Council of Troyes, in 1128, the papal legate approved the order. It was then headed by Hugh de Payens, the master of the temple. The knights wore a white robe with a red cross. The rule of the order was jealously guarded and the strictest secrecy was enforced in its deliberations. This secrecy later proved fatal to the holy knights.

The popes were well aware that they needed temporal strength to support their spiritual mission. In the Templars a well disciplined and utterly loyal army was at their disposal. In the bull *Omne datum optimum*, issued on the 29th of March 1139, Pope Innocent II granted the order unprecedented privileges, both spiritual and temporal.

The pope freed the knights of all ecclesiastical authority, except that of their own chaplains, and exempted them from all obligation to pay tithes. Their temporal possessions and castles were to be inviolable from any prince, king or emperor, and no one was allowed to demand homage from a Templar (Howarth 1982, 80).

The Knights Templar owed allegiance to the pope and to the pope alone. In effect they became a state within the state and a church within the church. Most of their wars were conducted in the Middle East, but the kings of Jerusalem had no control over them. The knights had their own castles, set their own policy, and even signed their own treaties. The rule of the Templars prohibited them to retreat unless outnumbered by more than three to one. The military-religious orders were the only standing armies in a feudal world, when vassals had to perform combat service only for a few months of the year.

Saladin, who had a well founded reputation for restraint, had nevertheless, after the battle of Hattin in 1187, all the Templars and Hospitalers beheaded in cold blood. In a sense, this was a tribute to the valiance and ferocity of the warrior monks.

After the loss of Jerusalem, King Richard of England sold the island of Cyprus to the Templars, but, after an uprising in 1192, they returned it. The island eventually ended up in the hands of Guy of Lusignan. In 1217 the Templars began to build their huge fortress of Castle Pilgrim near Acre. It was from there that the Fifth Crusade was launched against Egypt, which culminated in the capture of Damietta in 1219.

All of the great sovereign military-religious orders conducted independent policies and pursued separate alliances, which greatly weakened the crusader states' defenses. The military orders were always in competition with each other. In 1240 their rivalry erupted in open warfare. When the Hospitalers made a treaty with the sultan of Cairo, the Templars, who favored the sultan of Damascus, waged a bloody war against them, besieged their headquarters at Acre, and even drove out the Teutonic Knights. Peace among the holy knights was restored only in 1243.

With such savage rivalries among the pope's elite fighting forces, it is not surprising that the Christian armies were completely defeated by Bibars near Gaza in 1244. The grand masters of the Templars and Hospitalers both perished in the carnage. After Jerusalem was lost once more, Pope Innocent IV called for another crusade in which the knights had a prominent role.

St. Louis answered the call and, supported by the Templars, attacked Egypt. Only three Templars survived the battle of Mansura on the banks of the Nile. The king of France was captured and was released only after the holy knights advanced his ransom money. With the fall of

Acre, the last crusader stronghold in Palestine, the Templars sailed for Cyprus, never to return to the Middle East.

The power of the Templars was based not only on their sovereign military organization with their many castles and landed estates, but also on the fact that they were in those days the bankers of Europe. People entrusted them their money because they were knights with a strong military and naval power, and since they were also monks, they trusted their honesty. The Paris Temple, the order's European headquarters, was the world's financial hub, where kings and popes deposited their revenues.

With the end of the crusades, the Templars' military role as defenders of Christendom ceased. Their vast armed might was perceived as a threat by King Philip IV of France, who had no control over them; besides, their huge wealth wetted his appetite. In addition, when Philip, in 1305, applied for membership in the order, the knights, by a secret vote, refused his application. Even though a year later the king sought refuge in the Paris Temple from the violence of a mob, he treacherously plotted the destruction of his benefactors.

Royal agents accused the knights of heresy, idolatry, and sodomy, and ironically denounced them to another papal organ, the Inquisition. The grand inquisitor of France, a creature of the king, demanded their arrest by the civil power. The stage was thereby set for their dramatic fall.   Fearing the Templars military might, the king decided on a preemptive strike. On the 13th of October 1308 he ordered the arrest of all the members of the order in France. Under torture most of them broke down, and their confessions were submitted to Pope Clement V.

An intense public relations campaign discredited the activities of the knights, taking advantage of the strict secrecy of their rule and deliberations. The pope was at first incredulous, but failed to intervene. It was morally one of the darkest hours of the papacy. After two centuries of devoted faith, extreme hardship, and valiant fighting in the service of the Holy See, the Templars were abandoned by their supreme commander-in-chief.

Eventually, to regain control of the proceedings, the pope ordered all other sovereigns to arrest the Templars in their domains. Finally on the 3rd of April 1312 three thrones were erected at the Council of Vienne. "In the central one sat the pope; at his sides, and only slightly lower, sat King Philip of France and King Louis of Navarre, Philip's eldest son" (Howarth 1982, 305). At the session Clement V, "not without bitterness and sadness of heart" dissolved the order. The pope transferred the possessions of the Templars, not to the king of France, but to the Knights Hospitalers.

The Hospitalers (Knights of the Order of the Hospital of St. John of Jerusalem) were the first of the great military- religious orders to come into existence. Their origin was the hospital for pilgrims in Jerusalem even before the crusades. The hospital was expanded and showered with privileges after the capture of the city. The order was recognized in 1113 by Pope Pascal II, who took the possessions of the knights under his protection. Their charter was confirmed by Calixtus II in 1119.

It was under the second grand master, Raymond de Puy, that the society was reorganized into a powerful military force, although care of the sick always remained part of the knights mission. The order, which followed the rules of the Augustinian canons, amassed great wealth and obtained from various popes privileges that made it independent of spiritual and secular authorities, closely paralleling those of the Templars. The Hospitalers (also called the Knights of St. John) wore a black robe with a white cross.

In a short time, the knights acquired much land and strong castles, including Krak and Margat in Palestine. The great military power of the religious orders had the effect of weakening the power of the kingdom of Jerusalem, because they did not owe the same allegiance to the king as the feudal vassals, and often pursued independent policies. While the Hospitalers supported King Amalric I in his attack on Egypt in 1168, the Templars refused to cooperate on the ground it broke the treaty of peace.

With time the power of the orders grew even more. When King Baldwin V died in 1185, all the castles in the land were handed over to the custody of the holy knights. Although the military-religious orders played a leading role in all the crusades, the disputes and the wars they conducted among themselves were detrimental to the crusading movement.

An example was the feud from 1199 to 1231 between the Templars and the Hospitalers in regard to the claimants to the principality of Antioch. The two orders were also on opposite sides in the war between the Venetians and the Genoese that devastated Acre between 1256 and 1258. The Hospitalers even contemplated and alliance with the Assassins, for which Pope Gregory IX severely chastised them.

After the fall of Acre in 1291 and the expulsion of the crusaders from Palestine, the Knights Hospitalers captured Rhodes from the Byzantine Empire, in 1308, and ruled it as a sovereign power, minting their own coins and sending ambassadors to the courts of Europe.

On the orders of Pope Clement V, the knights enforced the commercial blockade of Egypt. Their galleys constantly patrolled the eastern Mediterranean. With papal authorization, they held up trading vessels suspected of illicit commerce and confiscated their cargo. This state of affairs ended in 1523, when Sultan Suleiman the Magnificent finally conquered the island.

The Emperor Charles V (King Charles I of Spain) thereupon invested the Hospitalers with the island of Malta and the fortress of Tripoli in order to protect the Spanish holdings in North Africa. Tripoli was lost in 1551, and the society from that time on became known as the Knights of Malta.

For a while the order continued to be one of the most formidable naval powers in the Mediterranean. In 1556 they put up a valiant defense, under Grand Master John La Valette, against a vastly superior Turkish invading force. Later they took part in the attack on Algiers in 1664, and helped the Spanish defend Oran in 1707.

As a result of the French revolutionary wars, the Knights of St. John lost their castles and landed estates in France, west of the Rhine, and in northern Italy. Napoleon Bonaparte, on his way to Egypt, took Malta in 1798, and swept away the last crusader state. The descendants of the heroes who fought under La Vallette were meekly expelled from their fortified possessions.

General Bonaparte's words clearly characterize the death of an age when, after reviewing the fortifications of the island, he remarked that the knights "possessed immense physical means of resistance, but no moral strength whatever" (Riley-Smith 1987, 256). Thus ended the last crusader state in 1798. In 1801 the pope appointed a grand master, but the mission of the order from then on was restricted to its original humanitarian activities.

The Teutonic Order (Knights of the Hospital of St. Mary of the Teutons) was the last of the great military-religious orders of chivalry to come into being during the Middle Ages. It traces its origins from the Third Crusade when German pilgrims to the Holy Land founded a hospital at Acre, which was later attached to the Church of Mary the Virgin in Jerusalem.

In 1198 the brethren were raised to a military order; a bull of Pope Celestine III confirmed their rights and privileges. Pope Innocent III gave them the rule of the Templars. They wore a white tunic with a black cross. The Teutonic Knights proved to be an elite force in the defense of the kingdom of Jerusalem, even though they were in fierce competition with the Templars and the Hospitalers.

Ironically, the Teutonic Knights reached the zenith of their power after the failure of the crusades, when they created a large state on the shores of the Baltic. It was Grand Master Hermann von Salza who established the knights as a first class military power. He was a friend of Emperor Frederick II, who bestowed generous gifts on the order, and raised the grand master to the rank of a prince of the empire.

In 1229 the Polish duke, Conrad of Mazovia, asked the knights for help against the heathen Prussians, and bestowed on them Kulmerland and whatever territory they conquered. This started a wave of Christianization and Germanization along the shores of the Baltic. Castles were built and towns were founded (Thorn, Kulm, Marienwerder, Elbing, Memel, Königsberg) and in 1308 their headquarters were moved to Marienburg on the Vistula.

To establish their complete independence, the knights in 1243 transferred all their possessions to the Holy See, and received them back as a papal fief. But only strong popes could assert any authority over them. The order ruled a large state as a sovereign power from Pomerania to the eastern Baltic.

The popes accorded the knights the privileges of crusaders. With the conquest of Estonia the sway of the holy warriors extended to the gulf of Finland. In 1263 Pope Urban IV granted them permission to trade, which transformed the order from a semi-monastic crusading society into a wealthy commercial enterprise.

The expansion of the knight's power was checked by a large Polish-Lithuanian force that defeated them at Tannenberg in 1410. By the second peace of Thorn, West Prussia, including Danzig, was incorporated into Poland. East Prussia became a fief of Poland, with the grand master being seated in the Polish diet. In 1525, during the Reformation, Grand Master Albert von Hohenzollern took the title of duke of Prussia and secularized the holdings of the order. Thus, the sovereignty of the Teutonic Knights over their Baltic empire came to an end.

During the Middle Ages, the three great orders of warrior monks comprised the elite forces of the pope's military might. They were in the forefront of the defense of the crusader states in the Middle East, in the attacks on North Africa, in the reconquest of Spain and Portugal, and in the conquest of the Baltic. The Hospitalers exercised sovereign powers over Rhodes, Malta, and Tripoli; the Templars, only fleetingly, over Cyprus; and the Teutonic Knights over Prussia, Livonia, and Estonia.

Their jealously guarded independence of all powers except the papal throne sometimes deteriorated into bloody conflicts among themselves, even when they were fighting on strange continents surrounded by enemies. Such actions were clearly counterproductive to the military objectives of the popes, to whom they all owed allegiance. Command without control is meaningless; the history of these orders illustrates this perfectly.

Chapter 5:

Dividing the Globe

As the European world expanded with the discoveries of the 15th and 16th centuries, the rulers of the continent naturally looked to the pope for confirmation of their claims, and for arbitration of potential conflicts. According to universally accepted international convention, the pope, as the regent of God on earth, held authority, not only over Christians, but over the entire world (Boorstin 1983, 248).

As early as the 9th century, Pope Nicholas I declared that the popes were set up as rulers over the whole earth (Ullmann 1965, 78). This view was seconded by the greatest of medieval popes, Innocent III, when he wrote to the patriarch of Constantinople that the Lord entrusted to Peter not only the universal church, but the government of the whole world (Kelly 1986, 186).

There were many instances of territorial judgments by the papal government. In 1059 Nicholas II invested the Norman leader, Robert Guiscard, with Apulia, Calabria, and Sicily. A century later, in 1154, Pope Adrian IV granted the overlordship of Ireland to Henry II of England. In 1297 Boniface VIII granted sovereignty over Sardinia and Corsica to the king of Aragon, (confirmed in 1323 by John XXII). During the 14th and 15th centuries the popes acted as arbitrators in the territorial disputes between the king of Poland the Teutonic Knights over the possession of Pomerania.

Appeal to the pope, the only universal and supranational authority in existence, was a normal way of establishing claims of sovereignty. As the vicar of God, his decrees were binding on all Christian monarchs. Traditionally, the pope allocated non-Christian lands to lay rulers, who in turn had the obligation to pacify and convert the natives. The situation was not unlike today, when contesting parties look to the United Nations to legitimize their actions.

Portugal and Castile appealed to the papal court for the first time in

1345 for a decision on the Canary Islands. Pope Clement VI granted the archipelago to Juan de la Cerda, a grandson of Alfonso X of Castille, and crowned him king of the Canaries in Avignon (Encyc. Brit. 1953, s.v. "Canary Islands").

In Africa, Portugal was the first Iberian country to consolidate its power and start exploring the western coastline of the continent. It took Ceuta in 1415, its first foothold in Africa. Prince Henry the Navigator's ships (he himself never went beyond Tangier) passed Cape Boyador in 1434.

Following these Portuguese activities, three papal bulls awarded the west coast of Africa to Portugal. In 1438 Pope Eugenius IV allowed the Portuguese to explore to the south. The wording of the papal bull was necessarily vague, because the geography was not known at the time. Pope Nicholas V in 1455 gave the Portuguese exclusive rights of exploration and conquest along the coast of Africa "all the way to the Indies" (as Asia was then known). Confirming these earlier arrangements, Sixtus IV in 1481 granted the Guinea coast of Africa to Portugal by papal bull.

Accordingly, in the same year, King John II founded a fortress and trading post in the Gulf of Guinea at Elmira, and in 1482 the Portuguese discovered the mouth of the Congo. Six years later Bartholomew Diaz rounded the Cape of Good Hope and explored the east coast of Africa.

When Columbus returned from his first voyage, a potential diplomatic controversy arose between Spain and Portugal. If Columbus reached "the Indies" by sailing west, how did this affect prior claims by Portugal based on the papal bull of 1455?

The Spanish sovereigns, Ferdinand and Isabella, immediately applied to Pope Alexander VI for a validation of their rights to the newly discovered territories. The pope, of the Spanish house of Borgia, obliged them by issuing a series of bulls that established a line of demarcation, from the north pole to the south pole, between the two powers.

The bull *Inter caetera*, issued by Pope Alexander VI and dated the 4th of June 1493, reads:

> We ... out of the fullness of our apostolic power ... give, grant, and assign to you and your heirs and successors, Kings of Castile and Leon, all islands and mainlands found and to be found ... one hundred leagues towards the west and south... from any of the islands commonly known as the Azores and Cape Verde (Commager 1935, 3).

The bull ends with the admonition: "Furthermore, under penalty of excommunication ... we strictly forbid all persons of whatsoever rank, even imperial and royal" to infringe on those rights (Commager 1935, 3). Portuguese claims east of the line of demarcation were left unchanged.

King John II of Portugal felt that the pope was too generous to Spain and, at a conference held at Tordesillas the following year, persuaded the Spanish monarchs to move the papal line of demarcation to 370 leagues west of the Cape Verde Islands.

The treaty of Tordesillas (7 June 1494) ends with a request to the pope. The kings

> entreat our most Holy Father that his holiness be pleased to confirm and approve the said agreement ... and that he order his bulls in regard to it to be issued ... with the tenor of this agreement incorporated therein, and that he lay his censures upon those who shall violate or oppose it (Commager 1935, 4).

The Treaty of Tordesillas was ratified by Pope Julius II on the 24th of January 1506.

The need for papal endorsement was just as important in those days as the quest for United Nations sanctions is today in international relations. Unilateral agreements can always be disregarded or violated by third parties. The line of demarcation was drawn at a time when the countries of the West still owed obedience to the papal throne, and when papal sanctions still had the force of law and acted as a deterrent.

In accordance with the papal bulls, Portugal established trading posts and fortifications along the west and east coasts of Africa and south Asia, and acquired naval dominance over the Indian Ocean. Vasco da Gamma bombarded Calicut in 1502 and defeated a large Arab fleet off the Malabar coast.

In 1505, Francisco de Almeida took Quiloa and Mombasa on the African coast, established forts at Calicut, Cananor and Cochin on the Malabar coast of India, and exacted tribute from native rulers. In 1507 he took Socotra and gained control of the entrance to the Red Sea. Later he dealt a devastating defeat to the Turkish, Egyptian and Indian navies in the battles of Chaul and Diu.

Francisco de Almeida was the first Portuguese viceroy of India, but it was his successor, Alfonso de Albuquerque who was responsible for

The Third Crown

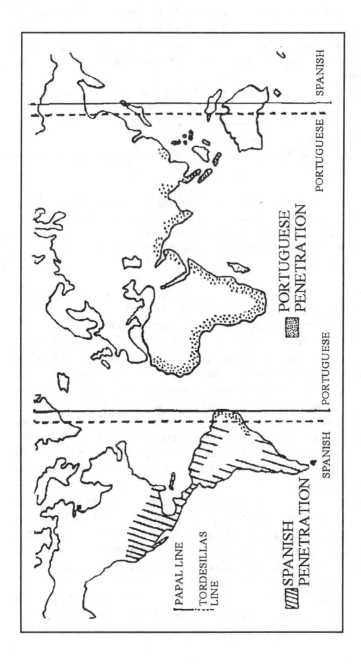

Map 5.1: The Line of Demarcation According to the Papal Bull of 1493

establishing the system of strong points which secured Portugal control of the orient as authorized by the series of papal bulls. It assured Portugal a lucrative trade for almost a century.

Albuquerque conquered Goa from the sultan of Bijapur and made it the main seat of Portuguese power. He took Malacca in 1511, securing the gateway to the South China Sea, sent expeditions to the Moluccas, and captured Ormuz in 1515, thus gaining control of the Persian Gulf.

Soon a string of fortified trading posts secured the coasts of east Africa, India and Ceylon, soon to be extended to Bengal and China. The Portuguese colony of Macao was established in 1557. The Portuguese navy was the master of the eastern seas, and the country's monopoly of trade with the orient was complete.

The papal bulls dividing the world had their intended effect. They eliminated serious conflicts among the European powers for almost a century, until the Protestant powers of England and Holland, spurning papal bulls, entered the scramble for colonies.

The Spanish conquests in the Americas followed swiftly after publication of the papal bull *Inter caetera*. Vasco Nunez de Balboa reached the Pacific Ocean in 1513 and claimed it for the king of Spain. Hernando Cortes conquered Mexico in 1521, and Francisco Pizarro subdued the Incas of Peru in 1532.

These vast territories, acquired in such a short time, were held to be, by virtue of the papal bull of 1493, to be the peculiar property of the sovereign. The papal grant of the Americas to Spain was confirmed by Pope Julius II in 1506, when he ratified the modified line of demarcation negotiated at Tordesillas, and in 1508, when he conceded universal patronage of the church in the Indies to the crown.

Pope Alexander VI's grant of the "Indies" to the crown of Castile was the founding charter of the Spanish Empire in America. King Ferdinand, who was very concerned about the legality of his conquests in the New World, had a document drawn up, called the Requisition (Spanish: Requerimiento). The wording of this document was the result of a meeting in the monastery of Valladolid, and reflected the thoughts of Juan Lopez de Palacios Rubios (Thomas 1993, 72).

The king ordered in 1513 this document to be translated and read to the native population before each conquest. It gave a short history of the world from the point of view of Christianity, and explained to the natives that the pope, as the regent of God on earth, donated their land to the Spanish crown, and called on the population to accept the rule of the king of Spain as the representative of the papacy.

As ordered, the Requisition was duly read by the captains of the *conquista* all over the continent. It was first read in Panama in 1514 by Rodrigo de Colmenares. Cortes had the pronouncement read in Mexico by a notary in 1519. At the conquest of Peru, after Pizarro read the document to the Capa Inca and his chiefs, the official report indicated that the natives had heard and "understood" the proclamation.

We know that at least two Cenu chiefs in what is now Colombia understood the gist of the document, because they commented, after Fernandez de Enciso had read it to them, that while they could accept one God who rules the universe, they felt that "the Pope must have been drunk" (Thomas 1993, 72) when he gave away their land.

The religious orders, especially the Franciscans, Dominicans, and Jesuits played a very important part in extending Spanish culture, and in developing agriculture and industry in the conquered territories. The church had a privileged position, and at the end of the colonial period it is estimated that it owned half of the productive land area. The Jesuit missions in Paraguay were politically the most important in the Americas; they were given complete authority and developed a governmental organization under a Father Superior at Candelaria.

With the discoveries and colonizations, the question naturally arose as to whether the natives could be considered on rational as well as moral grounds as full persons with self-governing and property rights. Of deciding importance was, of course, the position of the papacy. Popes Eugenius IV and Nicholas V, at the time of granting colonial rights to Portugal in Africa, accompanied their bulls with clauses to protect the natives from enslavement. The Medici Pope, Leo X, also decreed in 1521 that the Indians be properly treated (Thomas 1993, 539).

Consistent with these precedents, the bull *Sublimis Deus* by the Farnese pope, Paul III, issued in 1537, declared the American natives full-fledged persons capable of being converted and civilized. The papal pronouncements were reflected in the new laws of 1542, promulgated for the colonies by the Council of the Indies. They placed the population under the protection of the crown, prohibited their enslavement, and safeguarded their property. These humanistic views later prevailed in international law, but unfortunately were disregarded by early colonial administrators.

Pope Alexander VI, with his bull of 1493, in effect awarded America to Spain, and Africa and Asia to Portugal. The papal line of demarcation crossed the eastern bulge of Brazil. The treaty of

Tordesillas, however, moved the line further west, with the result that a large Brazilian territory was allocated to Portugal.

Since the line of demarcation was never surveyed, the Portuguese expansion continued way past the lands assigned to Portugal. In the Pacific, on the other hand, the Philippines, originally in the Portuguese sphere, were colonized by Spain. The treaty of Madrid in 1750, followed by the treaty of San Ildefonso in 1777, recognized these territorial deviations.

Francis I of France also had his eye on the New World and considered the line of demarcation as an affront to his country. He demanded "to see the clause in Adam's will which excludes France from the division of the world" (Thomas 1993, 569).

Despite French protestations, Emperor Charles V (King Charles I of Spain) remained adamant. He always maintained that the papal bull of 1493 gave him absolute dominion "beyond the line." When, however, the second Medici Pope, Clement VII, met with the French king in Marseilles in 1533, he interpreted the papal bulls as applying only to those territories already discovered by Spain (Morrison 1978, 171).

Pope Clement attended the marriage of his niece, Catarina de Medici, to the son of Francis I, the future Henry II. Clement was an affable pontiff, eager to cement family relationships. His opinion was a rather self-serving interpretation of the famous bull of Alexander VI, but it cleared the way for the voyage of Jacques Cartier to Canada in 1534. Later, Pope Paul III also raised no objections to further French exploration in North America.

The Portuguese eastern penetration reached all the way to Japan. In fact, the line of demarcation in the Pacific intersected the country. The Portuguese established trading centers on the island of Kyushu. Francis Xavier, papal legate to the Indies, landed there in 1549. The pope granted the Portuguese exclusive authority to conduct religious propaganda and to pursue trade in Japan.

The papal bulls of 1493 and 1506 placed China firmly in the Portuguese sphere of exploration and colonization. After the Portuguese took possession of the south Chinese port of Macao in 1557, they claimed, based on the papal decree, the monopoly of trade with China, which flowed primarily through the port of Canton. The Portuguese monopoly was not broken by other European powers until the middle of the 17th century.

By dividing the world among European powers, the papacy avoided many bloody conflicts between rulers competing for colonies. Basically, as Clement VII emphasized to Francis I when he granted French rights of colonization in North America, the papal "donation" simply referred to what has already been obtained under just title. The papal deed of gift to the kings of Spain and Portugal was an adjustment of claims among the powers concerned and other European princes.

The pope conferred a right of priority on these monarchs in regard to lands first discovered by them. To keep the peace, other predatory powers were warned away by ecclesiastical censure. The papal bulls were an effective means of ensuring peaceful colonization and of avoiding hostile encounters among European powers.

In parceling out areas of the globe, the pope acted in his capacity as a supranational world authority. His actions clearly parallels attempts by the United Nations to arbitrate claims to contested territories. In fact, one of the early acts of the United Nations General Assembly was the decision to partition Palestine into a Jewish and an Arab state.

The European colonization of the continents of the globe, first undertaken under papal auspices, started the long process of interaction among nations. It heralded the birth of the modern world.

Chapter 6:

A Supranational Legal System

After the disintegration of the Roman Empire, laws in many parts of Europe followed the dictates of custom, but customs varied from place to place. The popes as well as lay rulers demanded uniformity. For a universal governmental authority like the papacy, the need for universal, enforceable laws became a necessity. According to the generally accepted view of the Middle Ages, law had to reflect the will of God. Only the pope as a supranational authority had the power of issuing universal laws binding for all creation.

The first collection of decrees of church councils and of laws promulgated by the popes in their sovereign capacity as monarchs of the Christian commonwealth were made by Gratian around 1140. By the middle of the 12th century the *Decretum* of Gratian was accepted as the canon law of universal applicability. From Innocent III on the entire material was officially organized in law books, similar in structure to the *Corpus Juris Civilis*. The pope presided over a tribunal in Rome before which the whole of Europe came to plead.

The church registered birth and baptisms; performed marriages and burials; administered oaths; handled contracts and inheritances; protected widows, minors, and crusaders; and established hospitals and orphanages. Its courts handled all cases relating to these activities. The church legislated against usury and therefore affected economic life. In short, it performed many of the functions of the modern state.

In the 12th century the papacy emerged as a monarchical power on a universal scale. The papal chancellery became a central organ of government from which papal decrees were issued with universal validity and enforceability. After Gratian's collection, authoritative compilations of papal decretals were published by Gregory IX, Boniface VIII, Clement V, and John XXII. These remained important parts of the corpus of canon law and retained their validity until 1918.

Canon law claimed for the pope a formidable list of powers even in the political sphere. In the case of imperial elections, Innocent III asserted the power to judge the fitness of the candidates for office, and to decide disputed elections. He claimed the right to confirm and to pass judgment on treaties among sovereigns and to force contesting rulers to submit to arbitration. He claimed the right to exclude persons from office if they did not conform to accepted orthodoxy, to confiscate their property, and to discipline rulers who did not enforce the papal laws.

According to the canon lawyers, the pope held those powers outside and above feudal relationships, simply because of his plenitude of power. As Innocent IV explained:

> Though there are many offices and governments in the world, there can always be an appeal to the pope when necessary, whether the need arises from the law, because the judge is uncertain what decision he ought legally to give, or from fact, because there is no higher judge, or because inferior judges cannot execute their judgments, or are not willing to do justice as they ought (Sabine 1937, 272).

The pope did not deny the secular power's right to rule, he simply claimed a general power of review in all matters.

The unique characteristics of the legal system embodied in the Papal Commonwealth were its universal, world-wide applicability, and the idea that in the eyes of divine justice all men are equal. The canon lawyers transformed the pope's right to spiritual discipline into an enforceable universal law.

The papacy always had a legalistic outlook on the world, for how else could a universal sovereign govern the commonwealth. Medieval canon law dealt with all matters of importance and superseded all local laws. The canon lawyers claimed for the popes *regimen universale*, or universal dominion, which meant a certain superiority over the emperor and the kings of the world, and which made them occasionally champions against governmental despotism:

> there had been pontiffs whose fearlessness and justice were worthy of their exalted office, and whose interference was gratefully remembered by those who found no other helpers (Bryce 1889, 244).

The papacy gained control of international education by founding a large number of universities and of placing them directly under the supervision of the Holy See. One of the earliest universities and the most famous for its legal studies, both canon and civil, was the university of Bologna. In 1219, a bull of Pope Honorius III had already confered on it certain rights.

The University of Paris, which was recognized as a legal corporation by Pope Innocent III in 1211, was the center of medieval theology. It developed a philosophical system that exalted papal supremacy as the necessary foundation of human society. In the Middle Ages all universities needed papal or imperial endorsements for their degrees to have universal validity.

Egidius Colonna, author of *De Ecclesiastica Potestate* (1302), was one of the most famous exponents of the Papal Monarchy. He argued that there is no lawful exercise of civil authority unless he who holds it is subject to God, which means on earth to be subject to the pope. According to Egidius, "excommunication annuls law, contracts, property rights, and marriage, in short, the whole legal machinery on which society depends" (Sabine 1937, 275). Thus, the papacy used the law to recast the world on the papal model.

In the words of the Encyclopedia Britannica:

> papal decretals were often in themselves first-class juristic documents, endowed with universal validity and enforceability by virtue of the pope's function as supreme legislator and judge (Encyc. Brit. 1963, s.v. "Papacy").

One of the advantages of canon law, as opposed to Roman law, was that canon law was living law that could always be evolved in response to contemporary needs. In canon law the papacy codified an international legal system that was enforced in all countries of the West. Ecclesiastical courts decided all cases dealing with marriage, inheritance, oath, clerics, widows, minors, and crusaders. Papal judgements were binding and were enforced on all persons from sovereigns to serfs.

In medieval society no law could be valid that contravened the law of God, an axiom to which without exception everyone adhered. Popes did, indeed, annul civil laws that did not meet with their approval. The *Magna Carta*, issued in 1215, was immediately annulled by Pope Innocent III, because he, as the feudal overlord of England, was not consulted. The charter was later reissued several times with significant changes.

The *Sachsenspiegel*, the North German law book of about 1240 declared that the empire was held from God alone, not from the pope. Consequently it was declared null and void by Pope Gregory IX. The *Schwabenspiegel*, the South German law book, compiled half a century later, already clearly subordinated the emperor to the pope. (Bryce 1889, 108.)

To ensure ideological uniformity, the papacy in the 13th century created a special tribunal, the Inquisition. The episcopal inquisition developed earlier, but the papal Inquisition, administered by the Dominicans, was formally established in 1233 by Pope Gregory IX and expanded under Innocent IV. Heresy was considered treason against God and a threat to the established social order. The secular authority was instructed to execute the sentences of the ecclesiastical tribunals.

The popes were also concerned about the physical welfare of the people and took steps early on against the practice of slavery. Pope Sylvester II in 1001 proscribed the practice in Hungary, against considerable national pagan opposition. Gregory VII in 1076 when he bestowed the royal crown on Demetrius Zvonimir of Croatia made him swear, among other provisions, to abolish the slave trade.

Popes Eugenius IV and Nicholas V when granting colonial rights to Portugal in Africa accompanied their bulls with clauses protecting the natives from enslavement. Pope Paul III in his bull of 1530 decreed that the American natives are full fledged persons and cannot be enslaved. His views were duly incorporated in the New Laws promulgated for the colonies by the Spanish government.

During the Middle Ages, usury, the charging of interest for loans, was considered a sin and prohibited by canon law. This was a great obstacle to economic progress, and the need for change was undeniable. As time went on, especially after the great banking families of Italy (Piccolomini, Medici, Chigi, Odescalchi) attained the papal throne, the ban on interest could not be maintained.

Among the charitable institutions of the Middle Ages were establishments that lent money against valuables deposited as security. These were called the *Monti di Pieta*. Even though this practice was considered an act of charity, the need became more and more evident to charge a fee to cover the expenses. Consequently the Medici Pope, Leo X, at the fifth Lateran Council decreed that it is lawful for such institutions to charge a management fee (Creighton 1897, 5: 232). Thus, a first step was taken that allowed the evolution of modern capitalism.

For the popes, in their capacity of world monarchs, it was imperative to control the political process in individual countries. One of the ways the sovereign pontiffs dominated national rulers was by their jurisdiction over oaths. During the Investiture struggle, Gregory VII released the subjects of the German king, Henry IV, from their oath of allegiance. In 1105 Pope Paschal II, who supported the revolt of the future Henry V, released him from his oath of loyalty to his father. When Henry III of England submitted to his barons in a feud, Pope Honorius III granted him absolution to cancel his concessions.

Innocent IV, at the council of Lyons in 1245, when he deposed the Emperor Frederick II, also released his subjects from their oath of fealty. In 1305 Clement V released King Edward I of England from his vows, given earlier to his barons, in which he committed himself not to add non-feudal levies without a grant from parliament. During the wars against the Ottoman Empire, Pope Eugenius IV in 1443 authorized King Wladislaus (Ulaszlo) of Hungary to break his truce with the Sultan.

In dealing with ruling sovereigns, the popes always kept control firmly in their own hands. Innocent III severely rebuked the archbishop of Trondheim for removing the ban from the penitent King Haakon IV of Norvay, on the ground that the pope alone is competent to impose or lift sanctions on sovereigns.

Now every state has its own marriage laws, but during the past centuries, in every country of the West, there was a uniform law, the canon law of the church, which regulated marital relations. The highest court in matrimonial matters was the papal court in Rome. In regard to marriages, in some countries like Italy, canon law was the law of the land until the second half of the 20th century.

The power of the pope over monarchs was very often exercised through his control over marriages and divorces. The church "could alone solemnize a marriage, and if the church declared a marriage invalid, a disputed succession and a dynastic war were very likely to result" (Russell 1945, 395). Because the pope alone could decide the validity of a royal marriage, and thus the legitimacy of the offspring, he was in a position to control the succession to the throne.

Nicholas I (858-867) upheld the rights of Teutberga against her husband Lothair II of Lorraine, who wanted to divorce her and marry his mistress Waldrada. The pope's action ensured that the king's son by Waldrada, being illegitimate, was excluded from the succession. Gregory V in 996 excommunicated King Robert II of France and forced him to give up his uncanonical wife, Bertha. Alexander II also prevailed on the German king Henry IV in 1068 not to abandon his wife.

The papal courts also stepped in to regulate the succession to the crown of Jerusalem. When Isabella became heiress to the kingdom in 1190, she was abducted near Acre and brought before an ecclesiastical court. The papal legate declared her marriage to Humphrey of Tibnine invalid so that she could be married to Conrad of Montferrat, who then would become heir to the kingdom (Riley-Smith 1987, 115).

Pope Innocent III (1198-1216) firmly enforced canon law on the crowned heads of the continent. He forced Philip Augustus of France to take back his Danish wife, Ingeborg. He also compelled Peter of Aragon to give up his planned marriage to Bianca of Navarre, and got Alfonso IX of Leon to separate from his wife Berengaria of Castille, because of a too close relationship, but pronounced their children legitimate.

Alfonso III of Portugal, although he attained the government by papal sanction in 1246, fell out with the Holy See because of a bigamous marriage. In the end, Pope Urban IV legalized the king's domestic arrangement and legitimized his eldest son, Diniz.

The popes also used their legal power for political advantages. When Martin of Aragon, who supported the antipope "Clement VII" in Avignon, invaded Sicily in 1392 to claim the crown in the name of his wife Mary, the Roman pope, Boniface IX, declared his marriage null and void, because it fell within the prohibited degrees, and recognized Ladislas, Charles of Durazzo's son, as king.

Boniface IX, to further the political fortunes of his protégé, also granted a bull of divorce to Ladislas. His wife Costanza, however, was a spunky lady who later, when she was forced by circumstances to marry a local baron, exclaimed that her new husband was a lucky fellow to be allowed to practice adultery with a queen (Creighton 1897, 1:135).

Through his control of marital relationships, pope Innocent VIII had a hand in completing the royal dominions of France. Brittany was the last great fief not yet united to the crown. King Charles VIII realized that the most expeditious way to incorporate this territory was to marry Anne of Brittany.

One of the problems was that Anne, a girl of 13, was already secretly affianced to Maximilian, the future emperor. Another problem was that Charles VIII himself was betrothed to Maximilian's daughter, Margaret, a child of 10. Thus, papal dispensations were required on the grounds of previous contracts, and also because Anne stood within the prohibited degrees to Charles.

To cement his good relations with France, Innocent VIII issued the bulls of dispensation. There was no doubt of the historical importance of this event, and the rapprochement between France and the papacy left its desired impression on Ferdinand of Naples, who hastily agreed to pay the tribute due to Rome.

But this was not the end the affair. After Charles' death in 1498, Louis XII ascended the throne of France and immediately asked Pope Alexander VI not only to recognize his claim to the crown of Naples, but also to grant him an annulment of his marriage to Jean of France, so that he could marry Anne of Brittany, widow of his predecessor. The king, in turn, promised to find a princess for the pope's son, Cesare Borgia, duke of Valentinois.

A deal was made. Cesare Borgia soon arrived with the indispensable bulls of dispensation, authorizing the annulment and the marriage. King Louis, pleased with his new wife, wrote a candid letter of thanks to the pope, in which he proudly informed the Holy Father that he had "broken four lances" on his wedding night (Cloulas 1987, 161). The king also kept his part of the bargain, Cesare was married to Charlotte d'Albret, sister of the king of Navarre.

The greatest blow to papal authority following the Reformation was also caused by the application of canon law to the domestic relations of a ruling king. At first Pope Julius II had good relations with Henry VIII of England, and granted him dispensation in 1503 to marry his brother's widow, Catherine of Aragon. It was under Clement VII that the crisis arose, when Henry petitioned the pope for a divorce from Catherine, so that he could marry Anne Boleyn.

Since Catherine was the aunt of the Emperor Charles V, the pope was in a dilemma. He had just concluded an agreement with the emperor to their mutual benefit, and therefore was naturally reluctant to issue a decision against his aunt. In the end, the affair precipitated the collapse of papal power in England, and canon law ceased "to be an international code. Its study was forbidden in England by Henry VIII" (Binns 1995, 355).

As time went on and nationalism triumphed on the world scene, civil law slowly asserted its superiority over canon law. The national monarchies more and more exalted their own power and recognized no superior.

Chapter 7:

The Political Theory of Papal World Government

There are two basically opposing views of the origin of political power: the ascending (populist) theory and the descending (theocratic) theory. According to the former, power is vested in the people and delegated upward to their chosen representatives. In the latter view, all power comes from God and is flowing downward to the lowest official. At the present time, the populist view is holding sway in the world, but in much of human history it was the other way around.

For many centuries no one disputed the axiom that "there is no power but of God." The entire feudal system mirrored the descending concept of power. During the Middle Ages, every authority was invested "from above."

Since Peter received the power of binding and loosing on earth, the pope naturally regarded himself the apex of the feudal pyramid. It was axiomatic that only the pope could validly confer the imperial crown, and that only the pope or the emperor could promote a prince to royal rank. And so power was flowing downward all the way to the lowest official. Thus, The papacy emerged in the 12th century as a monarch on a universal scale.

This theocratic world view was reinforced by the fact that during the Middle Ages, when only clerics could read and write, education was in the hands of the clergy and almost all the chancelleries of kings and emperors were manned by clerics. The Christian Church was the dominant, unifying, all-pervasive organization in Europe, and no king could govern without the help of the ecclesiastical hierarchy. Separation of church and state was an unheard of concept until comparatively recently.

Kings rule over individual countries, small pieces of real estate of the earth's surface. Only two powers, the pope and the emperor, claimed universal sovereignty, but the emperor's power was in reality restricted to the territory of the empire.

Only the pope could issue a decree and, without dispatching a military expedition, prop up a throne or cause it to totter and often fall a thousand miles away. He could annul laws, contract, property rights, vows, and the fealty of a king's subjects. Papal decrees, on the other hand, could be annulled by no man, and cases called into the papal court could not be judged by any other authority.

The Fieschi pope, Innocent IV,

> took the papal power quite out of the categories of feudal dependence by asserting that the right to intervene or to supersede a negligent king was in no way dependent upon the king's being a vassal of the Pope (Sabine 1937, 272).

It depended solely on the pope's plenary powers. The pope's position in the European Christian commonwealth was the same as that of the emperor in Roman law. Looking at the historical precedents, the pontiff's right to depose an emperor or a king could be justified by quoting the Digest: "He who can lawfully bestow, can lawfully take away" (Sabine 1937, 237).

Popes considered their right and duty not only to remove unsuitable kings, but also to create kings, and not only for spiritual but also for secular reasons. As Innocent III remarked when he installed Kaloyan (Joannitza) as king of Bulgaria, he "wished to ensure the spiritual and temporal well-being of the Bulgarian kingdom" (Ullmann 1965, 112).

This did not mean that the papal government would supersede that of a king or emperor, only that the papal court would become a court of last resort on whose judgment a ruler's legitimacy would depend. In the Middle Ages, a government had to be Christian in order to be legitimate, and no one, whether king or peasant, challenged that proposition. Today, of course, the western world looks to democracy and respect for human rights as the guide to legitimacy in politics.

The papal organization was organically and constitutionally interwoven into every kingdom. Clerics performed most of the functions of the state. They also maintained schools, hospitals and orphanages. Ecclesiastical courts were in operation throughout Europe. Canon law controlled marriage and thus legitimacy, and was enforced in every country. Bishops and abbots sat in the assemblies of kings, and were often temporal rulers of ecclesiastical principalities.

The papacy constituted the world's first, and so far only, supranational government, and civil rulers acknowledged the papal throne as the fountain of legitimacy. They applied to the pope for the Roman imperial crown, and petitioned the Holy See for promotion to royal status.

The most powerful countries acknowledged the pope's right of arbitration. German electors, English barons, and Iberian sovereigns asked the pope for legal judgements. In fact, the kings of Spain and Portugal based the legitimacy of their rule over America, Africa and Asia on papal grants.

The western emperor was made, and sometimes unmade, by the pope, who looked at the emperor as his deputy invested with the sword to implement the papal plan of government. "The Emperor, indeed, could hardly be said to have any real authority or status until he had received papal recognition and his coronation in Rome" (Binns 1995, 55). As the fountainhead of imperial power, the papal throne towered above all political constellations of the world.

By the beginning of the 13th century, Pope Innocent III could claim with some justification, in a letter to Constantinople, that the Lord invested the pope with the government not only of the universal church but of the whole world (Kelly 1986, 186).

With the help of medieval political theory, papal authority was established throughout Europe, then, with the papal bulls of the 15th and 16th centuries, extended to the entire globe. During the high Middle Ages many popes had thorough legal training and formulated and expressed the legal authority of the Apostolic See with great precision. Both Innocent III and Innocent IV had first class legal minds.

When, after the disputed election of 1198, both candidates applied to the pope for the imperial crown, Innocent III justified his award of the empire to Otto of Brunswick in 1201 on the ground that while his opponent, Philip of Swabia, got most of the votes, Otto received the majority of the votes of those princes whose voices mattered most in these elections.

To streamline the election procedures, eventually seven imperial electors were recognized by two papal bulls issued by Urban IV in 1263. These seven princes were again designated by the Golden Bull of Charles IV in 1356. They were the archbishops of Mainz, Trier and Cologne, the king of Bohemia, the duke of Saxony, the markgraf of Brandenburg, and the count palatine of the Rhein.

As late as the Peace of Westphalia in 1648, Pope Innocent X protested against the establishment of an eighth electorate, probably because it diluted the power of the three ecclesiastical electors over whom the pope had a measure of control.

In the bull *Venerabilem* of 1202, Innocent III claimed that the pope in 800 transferred the Roman imperial crown from the Greeks to the Franks, and could transfer it again if he so chose. This is the famous theory of the "Translation of the Empire" that played such a decisive role in history.

The pope, therefore, reserved for himself the right to judge the candidate's fitness for the imperial office and to adjudicate contested or irregular elections. This bull of Innocent III was incorporated by Pope Gregory IX into the digest of the canon law, and became of great importance down to the 17th century

In actuality, the outcome of the election was only the creation of the German king (also called king of the Romans) whose royal coronation was performed at Aachen (Aix-la- Chapelle) by the archbishop of Mainz. But the German king also became emperor of the Holy Roman Empire if, and when, the pope promoted him to the imperial throne. Innocent III acknowledged that the imperial power came from God, but insisted that it can only be awarded by the pope as His vicar on earth.

Innocent III always maintained that the German king had no claim to the imperial crown, which was an apostolic favor. The king became Holy Roman emperor only after the pope confirmed and crowned him. The decision was up to the pope, otherwise he would have to crown a heretic or an imbecile. These views prevailed until the end of the Middle Ages. The popes' power to create emperors was always their most valued prerogative.

It is believed that originally the papal assertion of the right to dispose of the imperial crown in the West was based on the so-called "Donation of Constantine." According to this document, the first Christian emperor, when departing to his new capital on the Bosporus, invested Pope Silvester I with sovereignty over Italy and the western provinces. It was proved to be a forgery in the 15th century by Lorenzo Valla, but was accepted as genuine throughout the Middle Ages.

None of the canon lawyers, however, used the Donation as the mainstay of their arguments in defending the powers of the papacy. In fact, by this time the Donation had become a source of embarrassment rather than of strength; for had it not been held... that the Pope was the supreme disposer of earthly power, and such a gift on the part of the Emperor would have been presumption (Binns 1995, 309).

The Donation of Constantine represented the ideal of the future as a conjuration from the past. The underlying fact, however, was indisputable. The emperor, by abandoning Rome, left a political vacuum that only the pope, hallowed by his position and by his continuity with the Roman tradition, could fill.

In the view of the lawyers, the overriding authority of the pope was inherent in his powers of binding and loosing on earth. Basing their function on the regency of God, "the Popes could henceforward dispense with the Donation of Constantine, in which hitherto their claim to the royal part of their position was grounded" (Encyc. Brit. 1963, s.v. "Papacy").

The pope claimed universal government only as a fountainhead of legal power. Outside of the Papal States he did not claim direct government; that was the province of secular authorities. But he did insist on the right and duty of intervening in secular affairs when moral considerations required it. Such a general supervision over the behavior of states is, by the way, the definition of world government or, in papal parlance, *regimen universale.*

In his sovereign function, the pope exercised the right to declare treaties between kings null and void, to annul secular laws, to order kings to undertake military campaigns for a papal cause, to legitimize conquests, to compel belligerent parties to make peace, to absolve the subjects of an unfit ruler of their oath of fidelity, and even to transfer a country from one ruler to another if this were needed for the moral welfare of the commonwealth.

John of Salisbury, who wrote in the 12th century, was one of the best known medieval writers. His *Policraticus* was influential until the 16th century. For him the highest political organization was the all-embracing Papal Commonwealth. Because for medieval men the soul ruled the body, it naturally followed that the pope ruled the kings and set down the law that civil rulers had to observe and enforce.

Medieval thought presupposed a unitary organization of the

European commonwealth, headed by the priest-king of Rome, who was set over the nations and kingdoms, and from whose judgement there was no exemption.

As mentioned in the previous chapter, the political ideas of the canon lawyers received the most thorough presentation in the work *De Ecclesiastica Potestate* by Egidius Colonna, who is also known as Egidius Romanus. He wrote his tract in 1302 and it is evident that the bulls of Pope Boniface VIII relied heavily on the arguments contained in it.

According to Egidius the powers vested in the pope are unique and supreme and are inherent in the office and not dependent on the personal qualities of the holder. Egidius claimed that "the pope had sovereignty over the whole world" and that "unless subjected to him, no power was legitimately exercised" (Ullmann 1965, 124-125).

Although Egidius lists all the arguments in the legal and historical armory of the papacy, his main justification for the pope's universal authority is his plenitude of power. This is based on the superiority of spiritual over temporal authority, because, according to a doctrine first enunciated by Aristotle, the higher always governs and controls the lower by a law of nature.

These are the foundations of the political theory of papal world government. Through the decrees of Popes Innocent III, Innocent IV, and Gregory IX all these ideas were incorporated into the body of canon law. Throughout history, the papal government enforced its decrees through ecclesiastical, military, and sometimes commercial means.

The powers of the papacy were said to apply not only to Christians, but also to non-Christians. On the occasion of receiving the ambassadors of Philip Augustus of France, Innocent III expounded the superiority of the papal throne over all earthly authority:

> Single rulers have single provinces, and single kings single kingdoms; but Peter ... is pre-eminent over all, since he is Vicar of Him whose is ... the whole wide world and all that dwell therein   (Encyc. Brit. 1953, s.v. "Innocent").

Popes Innocent IV and Boniface VIII followed in their official pronouncements this line of reasoning, and maintained that every creature was to be subjected to the "vicar of the Creator." This theory gained practical importance in the 15th and 16th centuries when the popes parceled out the continents of the globe to European powers.

During the Middle Ages when most men could not read and write, political ideologies were very often embedded in rites and ceremonies that symbolically reflected the underlying program. The imperial coronation ceremony duly incorporated the papal doctrine in a symbolic way.

The candidate was first made a cleric. Before the crown was put on his head, he had to take an oath to the pope, promising fidelity and defense. The pope also girdled him with the sword, to symbolize that he wields the sword on papal command. The emperor also had to kiss the pope's feet, and had to hold the bridle and stirrup of the pope's horse.

From the 9th century on, royal coronations also took on a strong ecclesiastical complexion in their liturgy and symbolism. Kings stood below the emperor, so that popes only rarely performed royal coronations. These were usually delegated to bishops, who also consecrated the kings with holy oil. During the Middle Ages it was their actions alone that constituted the candidate a king.

As the coronation texts made clear, the king had the duty to promulgate the laws of the land, but those laws had to be consistent with divine law as set down by the church. The coronation oath had a religious significance and, like all oaths, fell within the jurisdiction of the pope.

With the dawning of the 9th century, we can see the step by step elevation of the papal governmental theme. While in 816 it was the pope who travelled to France to crown Louis I, seven years later it was Lothair I who undertook the journey to Rome to receive from the pope the imperial crown. This was the first time that the pontiff presented the emperor with the sword, the symbol of physical strength. The ceremony clearly established the emperor as an assistant of the pope for the implementation of the papal program.

By 850 the papal governmental theme progressed so far that the emperor requested the pope to crown his son Louis II, which was the sole constitutive act raising him to be emperor of the Romans. At this time the emperor-designate had to perform the symbolic menial task of leading the pope's horse the length of an arrow shot.

Considering these historical precedents, it is not surprising that Pope

Nicholas I (858-67) could assert that the popes were set up as sovereigns over the entire world whose decrees were binding on all and who distributed power on earth. Pope Adrian II (867-72) already expressed the theory, which matured under Gregory VII, that the pope has the right and duty to censure even a king, if he contravenes divine law.

The Emperor Louis II had already completely accepted the papal doctrine when in 871, in a communication to the Byzantine emperor, he claimed to have received his authority to rule from the Apostolic See. The papal program has finally reached its culmination in 875, when Pope John VIII by his own initiative selected and invested Charles the Bald with the imperial diadem.

Centuries later, the Caetani pope, Boniface VIII, insisted that the temporal sword was wielded by the emperor and by the kings "at the bidding and sufferance of the Pope," because a king's duty was to enforce the papal law.

These views were already presented by John of Salisbury earlier, but found their most extreme expression in the bull *Unam sanctam*, issued in 1302 by Boniface VIII. The document states that "the spiritual power must establish the temporal power and pass judgment on it" and that whoever resisted the pope's decrees, "resisteth the ordinance of God" (Viorst 1965, 68).

When Pope Boniface VIII clashed with Philip IV of France, the evolution of the national state reached the point when it could challenge the universal Papal Monarchy. It is ironic that the most exalted expression of omnipotent papal authority was coincident with its most dramatic failure as a practical policy. For the first time, the the pope's time- honored position as an international arbitral power came to be disputed.

During the feud of the Popes John XII and Clement VI with Louis the Bavarian, the papal theory of government was contested by William of Occam and Marsilio of Padua. They denied all papal claims in the secular sphere and tried to establish the principle that states are independent political entities. In line with this reasoning, the German electors, assembled at Rense in 1338, declared that their choice became both king and emperor and needed no papal confirmation. This was validated by the diet of Frankfurt with the law *Licet Juris* in the same year.

The change in attitude, however, matured slowly. The power of tradition and precedent prevailed for a long time afterwards. The writings of William of Occam and Marsilio of Padua were naturally banned by the pope. In 1346 Pope Clement VI declared Louis IV deposed and secured the election of his hand-picked candidate, Charles of Bohemia.

When Rupert was chosen German king in 1400, the electors requested formal approval from Pope Boniface IX. More than a century after Rense, Frederick III, elected in 1440, pledged the allegiance of Germany to Pope Nicholas V in return for the promise of the imperial crown.

Of great importance for the future of political theory was the decree *Pastoralis cura*, issued in 1313 by Boniface VIII's successor, Pope Clement V. It was a key document in transforming the hierarchical conception of the state system of Europe. The papal decree laid the legal groundwork for the equal sovereign powers of individual states within their territories (Ullmann 1965, 198).

The decree was the result of a feud between Emperor Henry VII and King Robert of Naples, who was summoned by the emperor to answer charges of high treason, and who applied to the pope for a judgement. Clement V completely reversed the traditional papal stand on the medieval concept of a feudal world order. In his decree the pope supported King Robert, who was his feudal vassal, by denying the emperor's right to cite the king before him to answer charges of treason because the king was not his subject.

Pope Clement argued that the king was sovereign in his kingdom, and therefore the emperor had no jurisdiction over him. Thus, for the first time, a decree by a supranational authority established the legal equality of independent states.

The universal authority of the pope still found powerful adherents as late as the 17th century. Cardinal Roberto Bellarmine was the most effective supporter of papal power of the period. He claimed that the pope alone among human rulers has his power directly from God and, therefore, has an indirect authority over temporal matters, exclusively for spiritual and moral ends.

The pope, writes Bellarmine, as supreme spiritual monarch "can change kingdoms, taking them from one ruler to bestow them on another; if this be needful to the welfare of souls" (Ranke, 1881, 2:6).

But by then a page had been turned in the book of history. The Papal Commonwealth that united Europe for centuries had been replaced by a new force, called nationalism, that shattered the old allegiances.

The last famous defender of the worldwide authority of the papal throne was Joseph de Maistre, ambassador of Sardinia to St. Petersburg, who wrote his most influential work, *Du Pape*, in 1817. He insisted that over all secular governments, at he head of all nations, must tower the absolute universal authority of the pope, if law and order is to prevail in the world.

The voice of de Maistre, however, was already drowned out by the clamor for the secular, national state. His work turned out to be an echo from the past, rather than the voice of the future.

Chapter 8:

Peacemaking and Peacekeeping

After experiencing the scourge of war, people were always yearning for the blessings of peace, but throughout history this goal remained elusive. In the Mediterranean basin the political unity of the Roman Empire could maintain for some time the *Pax Romana*. After the fall of the empire, the papacy slowly succeeded in establishing a sort of hegemony over the state system of Christian Europe and tried to replace, under papal rather than imperial auspices, the ancient dream of a peaceful world.

The popes traditionally have been in the forefront in ensuring and maintaining the peace and alleviating the horrors of war. The "Peace of God" was the first attempt by the church in the Middle Ages to mitigate the evils of private armed conflicts. It was first promulgated in France by various synods in 990, and forbade, under penalty of excommunication, acts of war against churches and noncombatants (clerics, pilgrims, merchants, women, and peasants). Ecclesiastical and secular authorities were vested with judicial power to enforce the Peace of God in their territories. In 1038 the archbishop of Bourges decreed that every man should take an oath to enforce the Peace of God and enter the diocesan militia. Also, bishops and abbots had their own retinues of knights and could move against disturbers of the public order to enforce the peace.

In the 11th century, out of the Peace of God evolved the "Truce of God." At first it prohibited military operations from Saturday night to Monday morning, but was soon extended from Wednesday evening to Monday morning and usually during Lent and Advent and on special holidays. The Truce of God was first recorded at the synod of Elne in 1027 and soon spread all over France.

Pope Benedict IX proclaimed the Truce of God at the synod of Marseilles in 1040 to control indiscriminate feudal warfare (Cheetham

1982, 84). It was extended to Burgundy in 1041. The bishop of Liege introduced it into Germany in 1082, and three years later the synod of Mainz, which was attended by Henry IV, extended it to the whole empire.

During the 11th century, the popes took firm control of the machinery of peacemaking. Pope Urban II at the Council of Clermont in 1095 extended the Truce of God to all of Europe. He no doubt felt that in order to unite the West for the assault on the Middle East he must first ensure peace on the continent. Pope Calixtus II again decreed the Truce of God at the Lateran Council in 1123. It was reaffirmed by Innocent II in 1139 and by Alexander III in 1179.

Eventually only about one quarter of the year remained for fighting. The popes enforced their decrees by ecclesiastical censures, like excommunication, by special tribunals, and by directing the secular power to implement them. At the Council of Clermont, Pope Urban II prescribed that the oath to abide by the truce should be taken every three years by all men over 12 years of age.

The Truce of God was the first significant attempt by a supranational authority to curb warfare. Although it was not invariably effective because "not everyone was prepared to fight to a timetable" (Howarth 1982, 23), the Truce of God introduced some brakes and humanity into the otherwise lawless society of the feudal period.

The papal peacemaking machinery reached the peak of its effectiveness in the 12th century. Later, as the kings consolidated their power over their feudal tenants, the king's peace replaced the peace of the church. The popes, however, continued their peacemaking efforts at a higher level by arbitrating conflicts between kings, and enshrined this power in canon law. The papal court became recognized as the agency of international arbitration.

One of the early peacemakers was Pope Leo I who in 452 dissuaded Attila the Hun from sacking Rome. Almost four centuries later, during the revolt of Emperor Louis I's sons against their father, Pope Gregory IV intervened with the object of maintaining the peace. When accused of meddling, he sternly rebuked his critics that the authority of the Apostolic See is supreme, and that it is his duty to ensure the unity and peace of the empire. (Kelly 1986, 102.)

When, late in the 10th century, Aethelred of England and Richard I of Normandy were on the verge of war, Pope John XIV stepped in and arranged a peaceful settlement of the conflict. The war between the sons of Robert Guiscard, Bohemond and Roger, for the succession of

Apulia and Calabria also ended with the mediation of Pope Urban II 1085.

The Knights Templar, one of the papal military orders founded during the crusades, were originally created as peacekeepers to protect the pilgrims and to guard the public roads in Palestine.

Today we have a number of international conventions banning chemical and biological weapons, and considerable efforts are undertaken by the United Nations to limit the spread of nuclear arsenals. These undertakings, however, are not as novel as many people believe.

In the Middle Ages when populations were sparse, infant mortality high, and disease and pestilence wiped out entire populations, the popes became conscious of the danger posed by potentially devastating weapons. Consequently, in 1139 Pope Innocent II issued a bull inderdicting the use of the crossbow and the poisoned arrow as weapons of war (Second Lateran Council, decision No. 29).

The peacemaking efforts of the popes continued with Alexander III when he intervened in 1177 in the conflict between Louis VII of France and Henry II of England and brokered the peace of Vitry. The large possessions of the kings of England in France was a constant source of friction between the two countries. Pope Innocent III also made numerous efforts to mediate the conflict between France and England, and in 1215 he proclaimed a four-year truce for all of Europe in preparation for the Fifth Crusade.

Since the pope had a special jurisdiction in maintaining peace among nations, Innocent III

> had claimed the power to confirm and adjudicate treaties and agreements between rulers, on the theory that the church had special jurisdiction over oaths; in effect this amounted to a general guardianship over war and peace and the right to oblige contesting parties to submit to arbitration (Sabine 1937, 271).

This, of course, was theory, and we all know the difference between theory and practice. But it worked often enough during the Middle Ages.

Pope Honorius III arbitrated in 1216 between Philip II of France and James I of Aragon to ensure the peace, and compelled France to abandon the invasion of England, which became a papal fief three years earlier. The campaign was originally authorized by Pope Innocent III, but after the submission of King John, was naturally cancelled. The

French troops and English rebels were excommunicated, and the future
Louis VIII, son of Philip Augustus, was forced to return to France.

Pope Gregory X was very much concerned about the incessant
warfare in the Balkans and the Aegean Sea between Charles of Anjou,
king of Sicily, who dreamt of the imperial crown of the Eastern Empire,
and the Byzantine Emperor Michael VIII Paleologus who, in 1274,
submitted to the pope to thwart the designs of Charles. The pope, for
whom Charles was growing too powerful, succeeded in arranging a
truce in 1275.

The papal peacemaking machinery went into high gear in the 13th
century. Popes John XXI and Nicholas III made efforts to restore the
peace between Alfonso X of Castile and Philip III of France, who both
claimed the throne of Navarre. Nicholas III continued to work for the
peace of Europe by maintaining the balance between the German king,
Rudolph of Habsburg, and the Sicilian king, Charles of Anjou. Papal
diplomacy progressed satisfactorily: Rudolph was to receive the imperial
crown and recognize Angevin rule in Sicily. Charles was to keep the
possession of Provence, but as an imperial fief.

To ensure the political equilibrium, the Orsini pope, Nicholas III,
reined in King Charles; he made him give up his positions of senator
of Rome and imperial vicar for Italy, and forbade him to attack
Constantinople (Norwich 1995, 240). The next pope, Martin IV (the
Frenchman Simon de Brion) was more sympathetic to the Angevin
plans in the east, but a Sicilian uprising intervened, inaugurated
Aragonese rule on the island, and ended Charles' dreams of empire.

The Caetani pope, Boniface VIII, who supported the Anjou claims
to Sicily, arranged the peace of 1295, by which James of Aragon agreed
to exchange the claim to Sicily for the investiture of Sardinia and
Corsica. The treaty also ended the French claims to Aragon. The truce
of 1298 between England and France was also brought about by the
mediation of Boniface VIII; it restored Guienne to Edward I of England.

Ironically, the first great conflict between Pope Boniface VIII and
King Philip IV of France, grew out of the peacemaking efforts of the
papacy. Boniface VIII wanted to end the war between England and
France. Since both countries taxed the clergy in pursuit of victory, the
pope issued in 1296 the bull *Clericos laicos* prohibiting royal taxation
of the clergy without the consent of the pope. England obeyed the
papal decree, but Philip retaliated by prohibiting the export of bullion
from France.

In the 14th century, the papal chancellery pressed on with

peacekeeping efforts. When Emperor Henry VII marched into Italy and came into conflict with King Robert of Naples, who was earlier appointed by Pope Clement V (1305-14) as imperial vicar in Italy, Clement threatened the emperor with ecclesiastical censures, if he failed to agree to an armistice.

As the clouds were gathering for another storm, Pope Benedict XII tried, unsuccessfully, to prevent the outbreak of the Hundred Years War (1337-1453) between England and France. This conflict was the result of the inheritance by the kings of England of the duchy of Aquitaine (through Eleanor, wife of Henry II) in the south of France.

The kings of France naturally wanted to unite this huge fief to the crown, while the kings of England just as naturally insisted on holding on to their possession. The war was an unmitigated disaster for both countries, and therefore it was expected of the popes to make strenuous attempts to end it.

Benedict's successor, Clement VI, succeeded in a limited way by bringing about the truce of Malestroit in 1343. Innocent VI, who followed Clement, invited plenipotentiaries from England and France to Avignon in 1355 in a vain attempt to avert the resumption of the War. Five years later, however, he succeeded in arranging the treaty of Bretigny, which ended the first phase of the conflict and provided a decade of peace.

When Pope Gregory XI was planning to return to Rome, his attempts at peace making between Edward III of England and Charles V of France kept him in Avignon. The only fruit of his efforts was a one-year truce in 1375. He was also asked to arbitrate a conflict between Louis I, duke of Anjou, and Peter IV of Aragon.

Papal mediations extended to the eastern part of Europe. In 1320 the Polish King Wladislaus I requested from Pope John XXII a judgment on the possession of Pomerania, which was also claimed by the Teutonic Knights. A year later an ecclesiastical tribunal confirmed the rights of Poland over the territory, but the knights appealed to the pope and eventually obtained a reversal of the judgment. Later, in 1346, Pope Clement IV intervened in the war between Poland and Bohemia and restored the peace.

Papal diplomacy in this period also labored to maintain peace in Hungary. After the death of Albert II in 1439, the Hungarian nobles elected Wladislaus (Ulaszlo) Jagiello to the throne, but he had to fight for many years against the supporters of his predecessor's widow, Elizabeth. As a result of a judgement by Pope Eugenius IV in 1443

Wladislaus I (Wladislaus III of Poland) was allowed to keep his throne so that he can lead a crusade against the Turks.

Before undertaking preparations for another campaign against the Ottoman Empire, the Piccolomini pope, Pius II, also arranged for peace in Hungary where the emperor, Frederick III, pressed his claim to the throne against Matthias, the son of John Hunyadi. In 1463 two papal legates arranged the terms which recognized Matthias as king, but in case he died childless the crown was to go to the second son of the emperor.

Three years later, the diplomacy of Pope Paul II facilitated the conclusion of another war between Poland and the Teutonic Order, which had been at that time under the papal ban. Hostilities ended in 1466 with the second peace of Thorn, through which Poland acquired west Prussia and an outlet to the sea. In 1582, papal diplomacy also helped end the war between Stephen Bathory, king of Poland, and Ivan the Terrible of Russia. It was negotiated by an emissary of Pope Gregory XIII.

It is true that some of the papal peacemaking efforts during the Middle Ages and the early modern period had the goal of uniting the western world against the threat of Islam. But this is a common phenomenon in history. The advent of nationalism tended to increase the power of kings. They very often achieved national unity by using the threat of an external enemy as the glue of social cohesion. As we all know, many politicians still practice this technique.

During the Renaissance, when the supranational powers of the papacy began to wane, a new mode of peacekeeping became necessary. In a cynical age, the old and overused papal enforcement methods of interdict and excommunication have began to wear thin, and eventually lost their effectiveness in international relations.

Many people believe that the concept of the balance of powers is a comparatively modern invention. In fact, it was an invention of the popes of the Renaissance. With the passing of the age of faith, disregard for papal decrees increased. To keep predatory states in check, the popes had to rely more and more on efforts to maintain the balance of powers first in Italy and later throughout Europe.

Pope Clement V, in deciding between the contending candidates (Charles of Valois and Henry of Luxemburg) for the imperial throne, always kept in mind the balance between France and Germany. In the middle of the 15th century, when Pius II had to choose between the two claimants to the throne of Naples, he selected, in the interest of the balance of powers in Italy, Alfonso V's son, Ferdinand I, over René I, duke of Anjou.

Until the 16th century, papal interventions were often effective, because papal decrees carried the weight of legal force and divine imperative. The partitioning of the globe by Pope Alexander VI in 1493, by drawing the line of demarcation between Spanish and Portuguese spheres of exploration and colonization, also had the intended effect of keeping the peace among the powers scrambling for colonies.

In view of the Turkish advance in the east, Pope Leo X in 1518 called for a five-year truce in Europe and dispatched legates to various countries to enforce it. The pope was to be recognized as arbiter of international disputes. All the major countries agreed in principle with the papal initiative, but not much was accomplished.

The papal task of pacifying the continent was never easy, because while the rulers of Europe paid verbal allegiance to the Prince of Peace, in reality they worshipped the god of war. They were constantly in pursuit of conquests and military glory.

Often perseverance paid off. The Aldobrandini pope, Clement VIII, was responsible for the negotiated peace in 1598 between France and Spain, which ended the last act of the French wars of religion. In the treaty, signed at Vervins, Philip II of Spain acknowledged Henry IV as the legitimate king of France. Clement VIII espoused good relations with the French king in order to counterbalance the overbearing power of Philip II.

Peacekeeping efforts continued by Gregory XV, who acted as arbiter in 1622 between France and Spain in the dispute over the strategically located Valtellina territory. He ordered the papal army to occupy the disputed lands to prevent another armed conflict.

Papal diplomacy was also instrumental in ending the Thirty-Years War in 1648. The papal nuncio, Fabio Chigi (later Pope Alexander VII) was the mediator at Münster, negotiating the peace of Westphalia. The treaty, however, severely restricted papal powers in Germany and was consequently denounced by Pope Innocent X.

The ascension of Louis XIV to the throne of France inaugurated a busy period for the papal chancellery. In 1668, after Louis XIV invaded the Spanish Netherlands, Pope Clement IX was recognized as mediator between Spain and France. The war ended with the peace of Aachen, but the period of calm did not last very long. In 1672 Louis XIV again attacked the Netherlands. The peace that eventually came out of the negotiations at Nymwegen and signed in 1678 and 1679 by France, the Netherlands, Spain, and the Holy Roman Empire was to a large extent the result of the efforts of Charles II of England and of Luigi Bevilacqua, the nuncio of Innocent XI.

The more secular atmosphere of the 18th century brought forth some ideas, independent of the papacy, proposing a federation of states and an international tribunal for the arbitration of disputes. The ideas of the Abbé de St. Pierre, Jeremy Bentham, and Immanuel Kant stand out in this regard. Some of these ideas came to fruition later and were codified in The Hague Peace Conferences in the late 19th and early 20th centuries, to be followed, after World Wars I and II, by the League of Nations and the United Nations, respectively.

Parallel with these developments, the popes continued their tradition of peace mediation. In 1885, after the reconciliation of Germany and the Vatican, Bismarck requested Pope Leo XIII to arbitrate the dispute between Germany and Spain that threatened a naval war over the possession of the Caroline Islands. The papal decision awarded the islands to Germany, with an indemnity to Spain.

The successful mediation and impartial judgment brought back to memory papal arbitrations of past centuries, especially that of Pope Alexander VI between Spain and Portugal. Voices were raised for a papal tribunal of international arbitration as an alternative to warfare (Gontard 1964, 520). The world, however, was changing fast, and the clock could not be turned back. The only other recent papal arbitration was by John Paul II when, at the request of both countries, he resolved the conflict between Argentina and Chile over the Beagle Channel.

Throughout history the papal government has engaged in the seemingly conflicting undertakings of peacekeeping and war making. But this is not as absurd as it appears at first sight. Any international organization engaged in peacekeeping will, under certain circumstances, have to resort to armed enforcement of its mandate.

Today, we do have an organization, the United Nations, charged with the peaceful settlement of international disputes. In addition to traditional peacekeeping missions, we have also seen armed conflicts under United Nations auspices, notably the Korean war (1950-52), the peace enforcement action in the Congo (1960), the Gulf war (1991), and the air action in Bosnia (1995).

Up to the present day, the popes have continued their calls for the peaceful resolution of international conflicts. Popes Paul VI and John Paul II by addressing the General Assembly of the United Nations, provided a fitting continuity to history. The torch had been passed to an organization whose mandate to arbitrate global discords is considered more relevant and legitimate in the modern world.

Chapter 9:

Can We Learn from the Past?

"Those who do not remember the past are condemned to relive it," said George Santayana. If we are to profit from past experience, we have to take a closer look at the successes and failures of the only government that in centuries past was charged with overseeing the behavior of states.

The concept of a universal presiding power that arbitrates conflicts among nations, maintains the peace, and is the fountain of international law always had a certain appeal for a large segment of mankind. In ages past, the papal government was the only institution capable of attaining such a position.

The 20th century has produced two world wars which resulted in an indiscriminate slaughter of about 87 million people. There is little doubt that closer cooperation on a global scale is necessary, if future calamities are to be avoided.

A future world authority on the papal model, however, is scarcely possible. Even a more democratic approach seems unlikely today, because the nation states still jealously guard their increasingly porous sovereignty, and also because more advanced nations will not subordinate themselves to a politically immature majority in a supranational body.

As we have seen in the preceding chapters, the popes for centuries past have embodied such an international presiding power

> especially charged to prevent strife between kingdoms, and to maintain the public order of Europe by being not only the fountain of international law, but also the judge in its causes and the enforcer of its sentences (Bryce 1889, 244).

In the judgement of Bryce, the popes were

excellently fitted for it by the respect which the sacredness of their office commanded; by their control of the tremendous weapons of excommunication and interdict; above all, by the exemption from those narrowing influences of place, or blood, or personal interest (Bryce 1889, 244).

The international community has already adopted many of the policies of the medieval papacy. In the words of the Encyclopedia Britannica,

As a universal authority the papacy in the 13th century was able to develop, apply and enforce a number of principles which have since become part of modern international law. These included the protection of legates and the safe conduct of ambassadors; respect for the sanctity of treaties; the humane treatment of prisoners and hostages; the protection of exiles; etc. By the same authority the papacy also ordered the free passage of troops engaged in a just campaign; instructed kings to enter into alliances; allotted occupied territory to a victorious belligerent; deposed rulers; and so forth (Encyc. Brit. 1963, s.v. "Papacy").

It is unlikely that any future world authority will again claim hegemony over sovereign states on the model of the medieval papal government. There is, however, one existing world organization, the United Nations, that is charged with maintaining international peace and security in the world. In fact, the United Nations has taken over some of the historic functions of the Papal Commonwealth. The two organizations have many characteristics in common, they both

Sponsored new nations
Arbitrated international disputes
Censured governments
Organized armed forces under their flag
Banned certain weapons
Took steps to maintain peace and control warfare
Allocated disputed territories

During the centuries preceding the modern age only the pope exercised authority over territorial rulers. It was he who invested the emperors and elevated princes to royal rank, and it was he who accepted a country into the community of western nations.

Today many territories attain independence under the tutelage of the United Nations, and receive recognition by being seated in the world organization. Some are even brought into existence by fiat of the United Nations, as in 1947 when the General Assembly called for the partition of Palestine into a Jewish and an Arab state.

During the Renaissance, when the awesome medieval powers of the papacy began to fade, the popes tried to keep the balance of powers so finely tuned that all sides would woo the Holy See to tip the balance in their favor. This applied to rival contenders to the imperial throne as well as to the power relations among the countries of Europe. Sovereigns did not object to the exalted claims of the papacy so long as they advanced their causes. This is one of the reasons that the popes maintained their dominant position long after they had lost the actual power to enforce their decrees.

A somewhat similar situation arose in our time in regard to the United Nations. Governments use the world organization to give legitimacy to their policies. It is significant that in 1950 President Truman sent American forces to Korea, not with congressional authorization, but based on resolutions of the United Nations Security Council. George Bush conducted the war against Iraq in 1991 with authorization from the United Nations.

Every organization needs leadership. "When the United States refused to lead, the U.N. did not know where to go" (Meisler 1995, 332). There is little doubt that without the decisive leadership of the United States, the aggressions of North Korea in 1950 and of Iraq in 1991 would have prevailed. Without a superpower's leadership, the United Nations is doomed to impotence. As U.N. Secretary General Boutros-Ghali once said, "I can do nothing. I have no army. I have no money. I have no experts. I am borrowing everything" (Meisler 1995, 291).

Medieval popes were seldom in such predicaments. The papal throne naturally represented a more efficient, though less democratic, mode of operation. Being a true executive power, it did not need the cooperation of five veto-wielding and mutually antagonistic colleagues to arrive at a decision and implement a policy. Although to a certain extent national intrigues were a constant feature at the papal court.

The most potent weapons in the papal armory -- excommunication, interdict, and deposition -- have now completely disappeared from the world scene. The papacy was the only authority in world history with the awesome power to remove a government by decree. Ecclesiastical censures, however, have lost both legitimacy and relevance in the modern world. Moral force still plays a role in world affairs, but it has no teeth.

Censures reflect the means and the spirit of the times. In the modern world economic sanctions are the most popular. United Nations did impose trade embargoes against countries that violated certain internationally recognized norms (Lybia, South Africa, Iraq, Yugoslavia, Haiti).

The papal government also used economic sanctions at different times. Gregory XI, for example, placed Florence under an interdict and ordered the goods of her merchants seized (Binns 1995, 187). Boniface VIII and Clement V even imposed a naval blockade on Egypt. Long experience has shown, however, that while sanctions do damage and frustrate opponents, they rarely accomplish their purpose. This was as true in the past as it is in the present.

In today's world the ultimate sanction is, of course, military action. It was also liberally employed by the popes for centuries in the form of crusades. In our time the United Nations used military force on a number of occasions (Congo, Korea, Iraq, Bosnia). In addition to peacekeeping operations, the United Nations charter also foresees armies under the command of the Security Council to impose peace on belligerents, although at present most nations are balking at this step of collective security.

Secretary General Boutros-Ghali conceded that the United Nations can carry out only very limited operations. Otherwise "the U.N. had to authorize others to do the job in its name" (Meisler 1995, 290). This is not unlike the pope's summons to kings in another age to execute a papal sentence. Earlier, the papacy provided the needed legitimacy. Today it seems that the Security Council's blessing for military operations of member states is becoming an important step to give those actions legal force.

While the popes, starting with Gregory VII, often did remove rulers from their thrones, the United Nations charter stands for nonintervention in the internal affairs of member states. There can be no doubt, however, that sometimes the censures of the world organization had the intended effect of changing the government (as in the cases of Rhodesia, South Africa, and Haiti).

During the Middle Ages, the popes first used the Truce of God to limit feudal warfare, and then established a solid tradition of mediating conflicts among states. The United Nations is trying its best to emulate that record. As of the end of 1995 a total of 73,400 United Nations blue helmets were on peacekeeping missions at 17 trouble spots in the world, at a cost of $3.6 billion a year (Meisler 1995, 334).

The world organization is also following in the footprints of Pope Innocent II in banning certain weapons of war. The United Nations Disarmament Commission is engaged in notable efforts to control nuclear, chemical, and biological weapons.

In reviewing the history of the Papal Commonwealth, several lessons stand out that may be worth remembering. Any world authority to be effective must be based on legitimacy. Legitimacy varies, of course, with time and place; it is different in a republic, a monarchy, or a theocracy. The medieval world order, however, was firmly founded on the descending theory of government, and people looked to the sovereign pontiff as the cornerstone of legitimacy.

When the pope called on the kings of Europe to maintain the peace or to join a crusade, or when he arbitrated conflicts or imposed censures on a government, these would have been futile exercises if the rulers would not have accepted the papal throne as a legitimate authority. The legitimacy of papal power went unquestioned for many centuries. It rested on moral authority rather than military strength. It needed no armament because it was inherent in the social structure.

Today we recognize as legitimate only a democratically constituted forum. Most governments today base their claim to rule not on divine right or dynastic succession, but on the will of the people. During the Middle Ages, however, all legal authority was derived from God. The pope could claim the allegiance of the western world because he was acknowledged as the regent of God on earth and represented the common ideals of peace and justice.

Another lesson that the history of the papal government can teach us is that formal legal pronouncements are worthless if they cannot be enforced. Politics is the art of the possible. Pope Innocent III, who exercised the powers of the papal world government to the fullest, was very well aware of this. As we have seen, before enunciating any public judgement, he asked three key questions: Is it beneficial? Is it legal? and Is it feasible?

A few of his successors, notably Boniface VIII (who feuded with Philip the Fair), Pius V (who deposed Queen Elizabeth I), and Innocent X (who declared the treaty of Westphalia null and void) had failed to ask the third question.

Issuing unenforceable decrees always results in loss of credibility.

One modern example was the creation of "safe zones" in Bosnia by the United Nations in 1995. Not only did the safe zones fall like a house of cards, the world organization at one point could not even protect its own peacekeepers. Such impotence is devastating for any world organization. As Boutros-Ghali remarked, "If you adopt a very practical resolution and the U.N., for different reasons, is not able to implement it, this will hurt the U.N" (Meisler 1995, 289).

In short, an organization charged with international arbitration must be based on legitimacy, and its decisions must be enforceable if it is to retain its credibility. For many centuries the papal government has met these criteria.

The halo of legitimacy and the possession of power, however, are not enough to maintain an organization's effectiveness. They must be exercised and driven home for constant reinforcement to take effect. We have seen how the papal government had used its rituals, especially the coronation ceremonies, to constantly reinforce the legitimacy of its authority. An international forum today can achieve the same results through its public relations activities.

Another lesson amplified by the history of the papal government is the importance of a unified command when conducting military operations. The collapse of papal policy in the Middle East was to a great extent the result of the conflicts among the kings leading the crusading armies, and the diverging policies of the sovereign military-religious orders (Templars, Hospitalers, and Teutonic Knights) which owed allegiance to the pope. It was the quarrels among the leaders of the crusades that nullified many of their victories.

In addition, a key reason for losing public support is the abuse of power. Censures generally lose moral force when used for purposes for which they were not intended. The pope jeopardized his credibility when he used ecclesiastical censures for political ends. The temptations were great, because bulls, no doubt, were cheaper than mercenaries. He also greatly undermined his position when he used spiritual sanctions for financial gain, as in the sale of indulgences.

Historians give various reasons for the fall of the Papal Commonwealth. The moral laxity of the Renaissance popes, their oppressive taxation, their use of spiritual weapons for political advantage and financial gain have undoubtedly contributed to the success of the Reformation. In the long run, however, the main reason for the decline of papal power was that the world was changing. The 17th century ended the last of the religious wars, and began to phase out religio- political systems as the foundations of states.

The 18th century launched the industrial revolution, which was a milestone in human history. Eventually, scientific advances led to the complete secularization of society, with the need to place international peace and security into the hands of an organization more in tune with the times.

The Security Council of the United Nations does have the power, which the defunct League of Nations lacked, to enforce its decisions and even launch military operations; provided, of course, that none of the permanent members uses its veto power.

The judicial arm of the United Nations, the International Court of Justice, however, has grave limitations. It is hampered by the fact that it cannot compel obedience to its verdicts. It is effective only if contesting parties agree to accept its judgments beforehand.

This stands in stark contrast to the papal court of centuries ago, which was

> the centre of a judicial and administrative system not only more efficient than any other government but the basis of all government. It was the final court of appeal in international dealing (Encyc. Brit. 1953, s.v. "Rom. Cath. Church").

The pope took it for granted that his values were universally applicable, and was striving for a global international order based on Christian principles. The western world has inherited this proselytizing zeal. Today we are attempting to establish a world order based on western- style democracy and human rights, and in the process are discovering "that historically conditioned ideas cannot fruitfully be transplanted on to a soil that has not been fertilized by the antecedent development" (Ullmann 1965, 231).

Examining how the universal Papal Monarchy has shaped the medieval world order may shed light on the problems and solutions of the present world. We have to remember the words of the historian Walter Ullmann that

> the governmental and political ideas dominant in the Middle Ages have created the very world which is ours. Our modern concepts, our modern institutions, our political obligations and constitutional ideas are either direct descendants of those in the Middle Ages, or have grown up in direct opposition to them (Ullmann 1965, 229).

For centuries the papal government had shaped the political constellations of the world, although it had its roots in spiritual and moral values. Even today ethical beliefs are closely connected to political structures in all societies, and are molding political concepts which are rooted deep in the historic soil. The past is never really laid to rest, but colors and inspires the present.

Appendix A:

List of Popes

From Zacharias, from whom the supranational authority of the papacy can be traced, to the fall of papal Rome under Pius IX. Names in italics are those of antipopes.

Reign Years	Papal Name	Original Name
741-752	Zacharias	
752-757	Stephen II	
757-767	Paul I	
767-768	*Constantine II*	
768-772	Stephen III	
772-795	Adrian I	
795-816	Leo III	
816-817	Stephen IV	
817-824	Paschal I	
824-827	Eugenius II	
827	Valentine	
827-844	Gregory IV	
844-847	Sergius II	
847-855	Leo IV	
855-858	Benedict III	
858-867	Nicholas I	
867-872	Adrian II	
872-882	John VIII	
882-884	Martin II	
884-885	Adrian III	
885-891	Stephen V	
891-896	Formosus	

Reign Years	*Papal Name*	*Original Name*
896	Boniface VI	
896-897	Stephen VI	
897	Romanus	
897	Theodore II	
898-900	John IX	
900-903	Benedict IV	
903	Leo V	
903-904	Christopher	
904-911	Sergius III	
911-913	Anastasius III	
913-914	Lando	
914-928	John X	
928	Leo VI	
928-931	Stephen VII	
931-936	John XI	
936-939	Leo VII	
939-942	Stephen VIII	
942-946	Martin III	
946-955	Agapetus II	
955-963	John XII	
963-965	Leo VIII	
965	Benedict V	
965-972	John XIII	
973-974	Benedict VI	
974	*Boniface VII*	
974-983	Benedict VII	
983-984	John XIV	Peter Canepanova
984-985	Boniface VII	
985-996	John XV	
996-999	Gregory V	Bruno of Carinthia
997-998	*John XVI*	John Philagathos
999-1003	Silvester II	Gerbert d'Aurillac
1003	John XVII	
1003-1009	John XVIII	
1009-1012	Sergius IV	
1012-1024	Benedict VIII	Theophylact of Tusculum
1024-1032	John XIX	Romanus of Tusculum
1032-1045	Benedict IX	Theophylact of Tusculum

Reign Years	*Papal Name*	*Original Name*
1045	*Silvester III*	
1045-1046	Gregory VI	John Gratian Pierleoni
1046-1047	Clement II	Suitger of Morsleben
1048	Damasus II	Poppo of Brixen
1049-1054	Leo IX	Bruno of Egisheim-Dagsburg
1055-1057	Victor II	Gebhard of Hirschberg
1057-1058	Stephen IX	Frederick of Lorraine
1058 1059	Benedict X	John di Velletri
1059-1061	Nicholas II	Gerhard of Burgundy
1061-1073	Alexander II	Anselmo da Baggio
1061-1064	*Honorius II*	Peter Cadalus
1073-1085	Gregory VII	Hildebrand of Soana
1084-1100	*Clement III*	
1086-1087	Victor III	Desiderius di Benevento
1088-1099	Urban II	Odo de Lagary
1099-1118	Paschal II	Ranieri di Bieda
1118-1119	Gelasius II	John Coniolo
1118-1121	*Gregory VIII*	
1119-1124	Calixtus II	Guido of Burgundy
1124-1130	Honorius II	Lamberto Scannabecchi
1124	*Celestine II*	Teobaldo Boccapecci
1130-1143	Innocent II	Gregorio Papareschi
1130-1138	*Anacletus II*	Pietro Pierleoni
1143-1144	Celestine II	Guido di Castello
1144-1145	Lucius II	Geraldo Caccianemici
1145-1153	Eugenius III	Bernardo Paganelli
1153-1154	Anastasius IV	Corrado della Subarra
1154-1159	Adrian IV	Nicholas Breakspeare
1159-1181	Alexander III	Orlando Bandinelli
1159-1164	*Victor IV*	Ottaviano of Monticelli
1164-1168	*Paschal III*	
1181-1185	Lucius III	Ubaldo Allucingoli
1185-1187	Urban III	Uberto Crivelli
1187	Gregory VIII	Alberto de Morra
1187-1191	Clement III	Paolo Scolari
1191-1198	Celestine III	Giacinto Boboni-Orsini
1198-1216	Innocent III	Lothario de Conti di Segni
1216-1227	Honorius III	Cencio Savelli

Reign Years	*Papal Name*	*Original Name*
1227-1241	Gregory IX	Ugolino de Conti di Segni
1241	Celstine IV	Goffredo Castiglione
1243-1254	Innocent IV	Sinibaldo Fieschi di Lavagna
1254-1261	Alexander IV	Rinaldo de Conti di Segni
1261-1264	Urban IV	Jacques Pantaléon
1265-1268	Clement IV	Guy Foulques
1271-1276	Gregory X	Tebaldo Visconti
1276	Innocent V	Pierre de Tarentaise
1276	Adrian V	Ottobono Fieschi di Lavagna
1276-1277	John XXI	Peter Rebuli-Giuliani
1277-1280	Nicholas III	Giovanni Caetano Orsini
1281-1285	Martin IV	Simon de Brion
1285-1287	Honorius IV	Giacomo Savelli
1288-1292	Nicholas IV	Girolamo Masci
1294	Celestine V	Pietro Angelari da Murrone
1294-1303	Boniface VIII	Benedetto Caetani
1303-1304	Benedict XI	Niccolo Boccasini
1305-1314	Clement V	Bertrand de Got
1316-1334	John XXII	Jacques Duèze
1334-1342	Benedict XII	Jacques Fournier
1342-1352	Clement VI	Pierre Roger de Beaufort
1352-1362	Innocent VI	Etienne Aubert
1362-1370	Urban V	Guillaume de Grimoard
1370-1378	Gregory XI	Pierre Roger de Beaufort
1378-1389	Urban VI	Bartolomeo Prignano
1378-1394	*Clement VII*	Robert of Geneva
1389-1404	Boniface IX	Pietro Tomacelli
1389-1424	*Benedict XIII*	Pedro de Luna
1404-1406	Innocent VII	Cosimo de Migliorati
1406-1415	Gregory XII	Angelo Correr
1409-1410	*Alexander V*	Pietro Philarghi
1410-1415	*John XXIII*	Baldassare Cossa
1417-1431	Martin V	Oddone Colonna
1423-1429	*Clement VIII*	Gil Sanches Munoz
1431-1447	Eugenius IV	Gabriele Condulmaro
1439-1449	*Felix V*	Amadeus VIII of Savoy
1447-1455	Nicholas V	Tomasso Parentucelli
1455-1458	Calixtus III	Alfonso de Borja (Borgia)

Reign Years	*Papal Name*	*Original Name*
1458-1464	Pius II	Enea Silvio Piccolomini
1464-1471	Paul II	Pietro Barbo
1471-1484	Sixtus IV	Francesco della Rovere
1484-1492	Innocent VIII	Giovanni Battista Cibo
1492-1503	Alexander VI	Rodrigo de Borgia
1503	Pius III	Francesco Piccolomini
1503-1513	Julius II	Giuliano della Rovere
1513-1521	Leo X	Giovanni de Medici
1522-1523	Adrian VI	Hadrian Florensz
1523-1534	Clement VII	Giulio de Medici
1534-1549	Paul III	Alessandro Farnese
1550-1555	Julius III	Giovanni del Monte
1555	Marcellus II	Marcello Cervini
1555-1559	Paul IV	Gian Pietro Carafa
1559-1565	Pius IV	Giovanni Angelo Medici
1566-1572	Pius V	Antonio Michele Ghislieri
1572-1585	Gregory XIII	Ugo Boncompagni
1585-1590	Sixtus V	Felice Peretti-Montalto
1590	Urban VII	Giambattista Castagna
1590-1591	Gregory XIV	Niccolo Sfondrati
1591	Innocent IX	Gian Antonio Fachinetti
1592-1605	Clement VIII	Ippolito Aldobrandini
1605	Leo IX	Alessandro de Medici-Ottaiano
1605-1621	Paul V	Camillo Borghese
1621-1623	Gregory XV	Alessandro Ludovisi
1623-1644	Urban VIII	Maffeo Barberini
1644-1655	Innocent X	Giambattista Pamfili
1655-1667	Alexander VII	Fabio Chigi
1667-1669	Clement IX	Giulio Rospigliosi
1670-1676	Clement X	Emilio Altieri
1676-1689	Innocent XI	Benedetto Odescalchi
1689-1691	Alexander VIII	Pietro Ottoboni
1691-1700	Innocent XII	Antonio Pignatelli
1700-1721	Clement XI	Gian Francesco Albani
1721-1724	Innocent XIII	Michelangelo de Conti
1724-1730	Benedict XIII	Pietro Francesco Orsini
1730-1740	Clement XII	Lorenzo Corsini
1740-1758	Benedict XIV	Prospero Lambertini

Reign Years	*Papal Name*	*Original Name*
1758-1769	Clement XIII	Carlo della Torre Rezzonico
1769-1774	Clement XIV	Lorenzo Ganganelli
1775-1799	Pius VI	Giovanni Angelo Braschi
1800-1823	Pius VII	Barnaba Chiaramonti
1823-1829	Leo XII	Annibale della Genga
1829-1830	Pius VIII	Francesco Castiglioni
1831-1846	Gregory XVI	Bartolomeo Cappellari
1846-1878	Pius IX	Giovanni Mastai-Ferretti

On the 20th of September 1870 Italian troops entered Rome, completing the unification of Italy. Thus, eleven centuries of papal sovereignty over the Roman States came to an end. With that, the pope stepped down from the stage of political world history.

Note: The break between Rome and Constantinople occurred in 1054. Between 1309 and 1378 the popes resided in Avignon. The Great Schism lasted from 1378 to 1408; some of the antipopes of this period also resided in Avignon. The Lateran Treaty of 1929 created the small but independent State of Vatican City, which restored the pope to temporal sovereignty.

Appendix B:

Chronology

751   Pope Zacharias authorized Pepin the Short to depose the Frankish king Childeric III and assume the crown himself.

756   Pope Stephen II, through the donation of Pepin, became ruler of the Papal States, which remained under papal sovereignty until 1870.

800   Pope Leo III bestowed the imperial crown on Charlemagne, creating the Holy Roman Empire.

850   Pope Leo IV crowned Louis II. He was the first emperor to acknowledge that he received his authority to rule from the Apostolic See.

875   Pope John VIII was arbiter of the imperial throne, selecting and investing first Charles II and then Charles III.

925   Pope John X bestowed the royal crown on Tomislav of Croatia, elevating the country to the status of a kingdom.

962   Pope John XII raised Otto I of Germany to the Roman imperial throne, reviving the empire.

992   Pope John XV was recognized by Prince Mieszko I as the feudal overlord of Poland.

1001   Pope Silvester II raised Hungary to the status of a kingdom by granting the royal crown to Stephen I (St. Stephen).

1016   Pope Benedict VIII launched a campaign against the Saracens on Sardinia and bestowed the island on the Republic of Pisa.

1025   Pope John XIX authorized the royal coronation of Boleslav I (the Brave) as first king of Poland.

1040   Pope Benedict IX was the first pontiff to proclaim the Truce of God. It was the first significant attempt by a supranational authority to curb feudal warfare.

1059   Pope Nicholas II invested the Norman leader Robert Guiscard with Apulia, Calabria, and Sicily under papal overlordship.

1066 Pope Alexander II received an appeal from William of Normandy for a judgment against King Harold of England. The pope approved the Norman conquest.

1068 Pope Alexander II was recognized as suzerain of the kingdom of Aragon by Sancho V.

1074 Pope Gregory VII was recognized by King Geza I as the overlord of Hungary, which assured the country's independence of the empire.

1076 Pope Gregory VII authorized the reinstitution of the royal dignity in Poland. Boleslav II was crowned king by papal legates, but was deposed by the pope three years later for the murder of the bishop of Cracow.

1076 Pope Gregory VII authorized the coronation of Demetrius Zvonimir as king of Croatia. He was crowned by a papal legate.

1077 Pope Gregory VII bestowed the royal crown on Mikhail of Serbia. He was crowned by a papal legate.

1077 Pope Gregory VII, in a conflict over investiture, deposed the German king Henry IV, who submitted at Canossa.

1093 Pope Urban II denied recognition of Peter Svacic of Croatia and invited King Koloman of Hungary to remove him from the throne. The crown of Croatia was united with that of Hungary.

1095 Pope Urban II proclaimed the First Crusade, which resulted in the conquest of Jerusalem.

1095 Pope Urban II proclaimed the Truce of God, limiting feudal warfare to certain days of the week, for all of Europe.

1100 Pope Paschal II authorized the assumption of the royal crown of Jerusalem by Baldwin I.

1113 Pope Paschal II approved the order of the Knights Hospitalers, the first of the sovereign military- religious orders of chivalry (the others were the Templars and the Teutonic Knights) which operated under papal charter and fought the pope's wars in Europe, Asia, and Africa.

1125 Pope Honorius II (Scannabecchi) supported Lothair II for the German throne. He was the first German king to ask for papal approval of his election.

1139 Pope Innocent II (Papareschi) issued the papal bull interdicting the use of the crossbow and the poisoned arrow as weapons of war.

1144 Pope Lucius II (Caccianemici) accepted Portugal as a fief of the Holy See.

1145 Pope Eugenius III (Paganelli), after the loss of Edessa, launched the Second Crusade, led by the kings of Germany and France.

1147 Pope Eugenius III authorized an extension of the crusade for the reconquest of Spain.

1151 Pope Eugenius III forbade the consecration of the son of King Stephen of England. The succession passed to Henry II.

1154 Pope Adrian IV (Breakspear), in his bull *Laudabiliter*, granted the overlordship over Ireland to Henry II of England.

1156 Pope Adrian IV recognized the royal title of William I of Sicily. It was awarded in 1130 to Roger II by the antipope "Anacletus II."

1177 Pope Alexander III (Bandinelli) intervened in the war between Louis VII of France and Henry II of England and arranged the peace of Vitry.

1179 Pope Alexander III granted Portugal, a papal fief since 1144, the status of an independent kingdom.

1187 Pope Gregory VIII (de Morra), learning of the loss of Jerusalem, launched the Third Crusade. It was led by the emperor and the kings of England and France.

1201 Pope Innocent III (Conti) arbitrated the elections in Germany and awarded the imperial crown to Otto of Brunswick (Otto IV).

1202 Pope Innocent III issued the bull *Venerabilem*, in which he asserted that the pope in 800 transferred the Roman imperial crown from the Greeks to the Franks and could transfer it again if he so chose.

1203 Pope Innocent III launched the Fourth Crusade, which led to the establishment of the Latin Empire of Constantinople.

1204 Pope Innocent III sent a royal crown to Kaloyan of Bulgaria. He became a vassal of the Holy See and was crowned by a papal legate.

1204 Pope Innocent III issued a crusader bull granting the same indulgences for the crusaders in the Baltic as for those going to Palestine, setting the stage for the conquest of Latvia, Livonia, and Estonia.

1210 Pope Innocent III declared Otto IV deposed from the imperial throne for invading papal territories.

1212 Pope Innocent III proclaimed a new Spanish crusade, which
      resulted in the great victory of Alfonso VIII of Castile over the
      Almohads at Las Navas de Tolosa.

1213 Pope Innocent III deposed King John of England, and
      authorized Philip Augustus of France to execute the sentence.
      King John submitted and was reinstated as a vassal of the
      Holy See.

1215 Pope Innocent III, at the Lateran Council, listened to rival
      claimants to the empire and awarded the throne to Frederick of
      Hohenstaufen.

1215 Pope Innocent III, at the Lateran Council, proclaimed the Fifth
      Crusade, and appointed the papal legate Pelagius as the
      military leader of the campaign.

1216 Pope Honorius III (Savelli) compelled France to abandon the
      invasion of England, which became a papal fief three years
      earlier.

1217 Pope Honorius III authorized the royal coronation of Stephan
      Nemanya II of Serbia.

1243 Pope Innocent IV (Fieschi) became the feudal suzerain of the
      Baltic possessions (Prussia and Livonia) of the Teutonic
      Knights.

1245 Pope Innocent IV decreed (at the Council of Lyon) the
      dethronement of Frederick II from both the Roman imperial
      throne and the royal throne of Sicily.

1245 Pope Innocent IV dethroned king Sancho II of Portugal for
      incompetence and awarded the crown to his brother, Alfonso
      II.

1245 Pope Innocent IV, hearing of the loss of Jerusalem, at the
      Council of Lyon proclaimed the Seventh Crusade. It was led
      by Louis IX (St. Louis) of France.

1253 Pope Innocent IV authorized the coronation of Mindaugas as
      the first and only king of Lithuania.

1262 Pope Urban IV (Pantaléon), after the fall of the Hohenstaufen,
      awarded the kingdom of Naples and Sicily to Charles of
      Anjou.

1273 Pope Gregory X (Visconti) ended the Great Interregnum in
      Germany by threatening to name an emperor. He proclaimed
      the papal candidate, Rudolph of Habsburg, king of the Romans
      at the Council of Lyon in 1274.

1295 Pope Boniface VIII authorized the reestablishment of the royal dignity in Poland. Przemysl was crowned king in Gniezno.

1297 Pope Boniface VIII (Caetani) granted sovereignty over Sardinia to James II of Aragon. The Aragonese took possession of the island in 1326.

1302 Pope Boniface VIII issued the bull *Unam sanctam*, which was the high point of papal claims of authority over the rulers of the world.

1307 Pope Clement V (de Got) ruled in favor of enthroning Charles Robert of Anjou (Charles I) as king of Hungary.

1309 Pope Clement V transferred the papal court to Avignon, which in 1348 became a papal possession. Avignon remained the seat of the papacy until 1367.

1313 Pope Clement V issued the bull *Pastoralis cura*. It was the first pronouncement by a supranational authority that circumvented feudal relationships and established the legal equality of sovereign states.

1320 Pope John XXII authorized the reinstitution of the royal dignity in Poland. Wladislaus I, after having reunified the country, received the royal crown.

1345 Pope Clement VI (de Beaufort) awarded the Canary Islands to Juan de la Cerda, grandson of Alfonso X of Castile, and crowned him king of the Canaries in Avignon.

1346 Pope Clement VI ordered the deposition of Louis IV from the imperial throne. The German princes elected the papal candidate Charles of Bohemia.

1380 Pope Urban VI (Prignano), under whom the Great Schism began, deposed Queen Joanna of Naples and installed Charles of Durazzo (Charles III) as king.

1390 Pope Boniface IX (Tomacelli) enfeoffed Ladislas, the son of Charles III, with the kingdom of Naples.

1402 Pope Boniface IX declared (in secret consistory) Ladislas of Naples king of Hungary. He was crowned at Zara, but was defeated in Hungary.

1455 Pope Nicholas V (Parentucelli) gave Portugal exclusive rights of exploration and conquest along the coast of Africa.

1466 Pope Paul II (Barbo) deposed King George (Podiebrad) from the throne of Bohemia. As a result the Catholic party elected Matthias of Hungary.

1481   Pope Sixtus IV (della Rovere) granted the Guinea coast of
       Africa to Portugal by papal bull.

1493   Pope Alexander VI (Borgia) issued the papal bull *Inter
       caetera*, dividing the globe between Spanish and Portuguese
       colonial spheres. The pope, in effect, awarded America to
       Spain and Africa and Asia to Portugal.

1506   Pope Julius II (della Rovere) ratified the Treaty of Tordesillas
       of 1494, moving the papal line of demarcation between the
       Spanish and Portuguese colonial spheres to 370 leagues west
       of the Cape Verde Islands.

1508   Pope Julius II granted to Maximilian I the title "Roman
       emperor-elect," which succeeding German kings assumed at
       their election.

1510   Pope Julius II, rejecting French claims, enfeoffed Ferdinand II
       of Aragon with the kingdom of Naples.

1520   Pope Leo X (Medici) issued the bull banning Martin Luther,
       precipitating the Reformation and the wars of religion.

1530   Pope Clement VII (Medici) crowned Charles V in Bologna.
       This was the last investiture of a Holy Roman emperor by a
       pope.

1533   Pope Clement VII excommunicated Henry VIII of England
       and pronounced his divorce and remarriage null and void. The
       king became head of the Church of England.

1570   Pope Pius V (Ghislieri) issued the bull *Regnans in excelsis*,
       deposing Queen Elizabeth I from the throne of England. Philip
       II of Spain heeded the call to execute the sentence, but the
       destruction of the Spanish Armada in 1588 saved the throne of
       the Virgin Queen.

1571   Pope Pius V formed a Holy League against the Ottoman
       Empire, completely destroying the Turkish fleet at Lepanto.

1582   Pope Gregory XIII (Boncompagni) issued the papal bull
       ordering the reform of the Julian calendar. The Gregorian
       calendar, named after him, is now in use.

1595   Pope Clement VIII (Aldobrandini) lifted the ban from Henry
       of Navarre and recognized him as the rightful king of France,
       bringing to a close the French wars of religion.

1598   Pope Clement VIII arranged the peace of Vervins between
       Philip II of Spain and Henry IV of France.

1684 Pope Innocent XI (Odescalchi) organized a Holy League against the Ottoman Empire. The league liberated Hungary and ended the Turkish threat to Europe.

1804 Pope Pius VII (Chiaramonti) consecrated Napoleon I emperor of the French in Paris.

1870 Pope Pius IX (Mastai-Ferretti) surrendered Rome to King Victor Emmanuel of Italy, ending eleven centuries if papal sovereignty over the Roman States.

Appendix C:

Holy Roman Emperors Invested by Popes

The name in italics is that of an antipope.

Emperor	Year	Crowned by
Charlemagne	800	Leo III
Louis I	816	Stephen IV
Lothair I	823	Paschal I
Louis II	850	Leo IV
Charles II	875	John VIII
Charles III	881	John VIII
Guido	891	Stephen V
Lambert	891	Stephen V
Arnulf	896	Formosus
Louis III	901	Benedict IV
Berengar	915	John X
Otto I	962	John XII
Otto II	967	John XIII
Otto III	996	Gregory V
Henry II	1014	Benedict VIII
Conrad II	1027	John XIX
Henry III	1046	Clement II
Henry IV	1084	*Clement III*
Henry V	1111	Paschal II
Lothair II	1133	Innocent II
Conrad III	German king only	
Frederick I	1155	Adrian IV
Henry VI	1191	Celestin III
Otto IV	1209	Innocent III
Frederick II	1220	Honorius III

Emperor	Year	Crowned by Pope
Conrad IV	German king only	
Rudolph I	German king only	
Adolph I	German king only	
Albert I	German king only	
Henry VII	1312	Papal Legate
Louis IV	1328	Lay coronation
Charles IV	1355	Papal Legate
Wenceslas	German king only	
Rupert	German king only	
Sigismund	1433	Eugenius IV
Albert II	German king only	
Frederick III	1452	Nicholas V
Maximilian I	Emperor-elect	
Charles V	1530	Clement VII

Unless crowned emperor by the pope, German kings bore the misleading title of "king of the Romans." In 1508 Pope Julius II granted Maximilian I the title of "Roman emperor-elect." After Charles V, until the dissolution of the empire in 1806, all German kings assumed this title. Rome was, of course, the capital of the Papal States and not even part of the empire to which it lent its name.

Appendix D:

Major Crusades Proclaimed by Popes

Years designate the date of proclamation, not the start of a campaign.

Military Operation	Year	Proclaimed by
First Crusade for the conquest of Jerusalem	1095	Urban II
Second Crusade, launched after loss of Edessa	1145	Eugenius III
Crusade in Spain vs the Moors	1147	Eugenius III
Third Crusade, launched after loss of Jerusalem	1187	Gregory VIII
Fourth Crusade, resulting in conquest of Constantinople	1202	Innocent III
Crusade in the Baltic for the conquest of Livonia	1204	Innocent III
Crusade vs Albigensians	1208	Innocent III
Crusade in Spain, resulting in victory at Tolosa	1212	Innocent III
Fifth Crusade, attacking Egypt	1215	Innocent III
Sixth Crusade	(Negotiated Settlement)	
Crusade vs Emperor Frederick II	1239	Gregory IX
Crusade vs Mongols to halt their invasion	1241	Gregory IX

Military Operation	Year	Proclaimed by
Seventh Crusade, attacking Egypt	1245	Innocent IV
Crusade in the Baltic to help Teutonic Knights	1245	Innocent IV
Crusade in Spain, resulting in reconquest of Seville	1246	Innocent IV
Crusade vs Turks, ending in defeat at Nicopolis	1394	Boniface IX
Crusade vs Hussites	1420	Martin V
Crusade vs Turks, ending in defeat at Varna	1443	Eugenius IV
Holy League vs Turks, resulting in victory at Lepanto	1571	Pius V
Holy League vs Turks, resulting in liberation of Hungary	1684	Innocent XI

Appendix E:

Major Universities Established by Popes

During the Middle Ages universities needed papal or imperial endorsements for their diplomas to have universal validity. Names in italics are those of antipopes.

University at	Year	Bull of Recognition by
Paris	1211	Innocent III
Oxford	1214	Innocent III
Bologna	1219	Honorius III
Padua	1222	Honorius III
Cambridge	1233	Gregory IX
Toulouse	1233	Gregory IX
Piacenza	1248	Innocent IV
Montpellier	1289	Nicholas IV
Lisbon	1290	Nicholas IV
Rome	1303	Boniface VIII
Orleans	1305	Clement V
Perugia	1307	Clement V
Pisa	1343	Clement VI
Valladolid	1346	Clement VI
Prague	1347	Clement VI
Florence	1349	Clement VI
Cracow	1364	Urban V
Vienna	1365	Urban V
Heidelberg	1385	Urban VI
Cologne	1388	Urban VI
Erfurt	1389	Urban VI
Leipzig	1409	*Alexander V*

University at	*Year*	*Bull of Recognition by*
St.Andrews	1413	*Benedict XIII*
Caen	1437	Eugenius IV
Trier	1450	Nicholas V
Glasgow	1451	Nicholas V
Rostock	1456	Calixtus III
Basle	1459	Pius II
Mainz	1476	Sixtus IV
Copenhagen	1475	Sixtus IV
Uppsala	1477	Sixtus IV
Aberdeen	1494	Alexander VI
Seville	1505	Julius II
Santiago	1526	Clement VII
Orviedo	1574	Gregory XIII
Manila	1645	Innocent X
Guatemala	1676	Innocent XI

Bibliography

Auchincloss, Louis. *Richelieu*, New York: Viking Press, 1972.

Binns, L. Elliott. *The Decline and Fall of the Medieval Papacy*. New York; Barnes and Noble Books, 1995.

Bishop, Morris. *The Middle Ages*. Boston: Houghton Mifflin Company, 1968.

Boorstin, Daniel J. *The Discoverers*. New York: Vintage Books, 1983.

Brown, R. Allen. *The Origins of Modern Europe*. New York: Barnes and Noble Books, 1972.

Bryce, James. *The Holy Roman Empire*. London: Macmillan and Company, 1889.

Cambridge Medieval History, 8 vols.. New York: Cambridge University Press, 1964.

Cantor, Norman F. *The Medieval World*. New York: Macmillan Company, 1963.

Cheetham, Nicholas. *A History of the Popes*. New York: Barnes and Noble, 1982.

Chamber's Encyclopedia. London: International Learning Systems, Inc., 1966.

Clough, Shepard B., ed. *A History of the Western World*, 2d ed., 2 vols.. Lexington, Mass.: D.C. Heath and Company, 1969.

Cloulas, Ivan. *The Borgias*. New York: Barnes and Noble, 1987.

Commager, Henry Steele. *Documents of American History*. New York: F.S. Crofts and Company, 1935.

Creighton, M. *A History of the Papacy*, 6 vols.. London: Longmans, Green, and Company, 1897.

De Rosa, Peter. *Vicars of Christ*. New York: Crown Publishers, 1988.

Douglas, David C. *William the Conqueror*. University of California Press, 1964.

Encyclopedia Britannica. 1953 and 1963 Editions.

Fernandez-Armesto, Felipe. *Columbus*. Oxford: Oxford
    University Press, 1992.
Fraknoi, Vilmos. *XI Incze Pápa*. Budapest: Szent István
    Tarsulat, 1886.
Gibbon, Edward. *The History of the Decline and Fall of the
    Roman Empire*, 6 vols.. Boston: Phillips, Sampson and
    Company, 1885.
Gibbon, Edward. *The Decline and Fall of the Roman Empire*
    (Abr.). New York: Harcourt, Brace and Company, 1960.
Gontard, Friedrich. *The Chair of Peter*. New York: Holt,
    Rinehart and Winston, 1964.
Halecki, O. *A History of Poland*. New York: David McKay
    Company, Inc., 1976.
Hanson, Eric O. *The Catholic Church in World Politics*.
    Princeton: Princeton University Press, 1987.
Hemming, John. *The Conquest of the Incas*. San Diego: A
    Harvest Book, Harcourt, Brace and Company, 1970.
History of the Western World, 2 vols.. Lexington, Mass.:
    D.C. Heath and Company, 1969.
Holborn, Hajo. *History of Modern Germany: The Reformation*.
    New York: Alfred A. Knopf, 1961.
Howarth, Stephen. *The Knights Templar*. New York: Dorset
    Press, 1982.
Kelly, J.N.D. *The Oxford Dictionary of Popes*. Oxford and New
    York: Oxford University Press, 1986.
Kuehner, Hans. *Lexikon der Päpste*. Frankfurt-am-Main: Fisher
    Bücherei, 1960.
Langer, William L. *An Encyclopedia of World History*. Boston:
    Houghton Mifflin Company, 1984.
Lefebvre, George. *Napoleon: From 18 Brumaire to Tilsit*. New
    York: Columbia University Press, 1969.
Lyon, Bryce D. *The High Middle Ages*. Toronto: The Free Press
    of Glencoe, Collier-Macmillan Ltd, 1964.
Meisler, Stanley. *United Nations*. New York: The Atlantic
    Monthly Press, 1995.
Morrison, S. E. *The Great Explorers*. New York: Oxford
    University Press, 1978.
Norvich, John Julius. *Byzantium: The Early Centuries*.
    New York, Alfred A. Knopf, 1989.

Norwich, John Julius. *Byzantium: The Decline and Fall.* New York: Alfred A Knopf, 1995.

Ogg, David. *Europe in the Seventeenth Century.* New York: Collier Books, 1960.

Ranke, Leopold von. *History of the Popes,* 3 vols.. London: George Bell and Sons, 1881.

Riley-Smith, Jonathan. *The Crusades.* New Haven and London: Yale University Press, 1987.

Russell, Bertrand. *A History of Western Philosophy.* New York: Simon and Schuster, 1945.

Sabine, George H. *A History of Political Theory.* New York: Henry Holt and Company, 1937.

Thomas, Hugh. *Conquest.* New York: Simon an Schuster, Touchstone Books, 1993.

Translations and Reprints from the Original Sources of European History, 6 vols.. Philadelphia: University of Pennsylvania, 1902.

Tuchman, Barbara W. *The March of Folly.* New York: Alfred A. Knopf, 1984.

Ullmann, Walter. *A History of Political Thought: The Middle Ages.* Baltimore: Penguin Books, 1965.

Valentin, Veit. *Welt Geschichte.* Gütersloh: Bertelsmann-Lesering, 1939.

Viorst, Milton. *The Great Documents of Western Civilization.* New York: Bantam Books, 1965.

INDEX